KABBALISTIC
TAROT

KABBALISTIC TAROT

Hebraic Wisdom in the Major and Minor Arcana

Dovid Krafchow

Inner Traditions
Rochester, Vermont

Inner Traditions
One Park Street
Rochester, Vermont 05767
www.InnerTraditions.com

LIBRARY OF CONGRESS CATALOGING-IN-PUBLICATION DATA

Krafchow, Dovid.
Kabbalistic tarot : Hebraic wisdom in the major and minor
arcana / Dovid Krafchow.
p. cm.
ISBN 978-1-59477-064-7
1. Tarot. 2. Cabala. I. Title.
BF1879.T2K72 2005
133.3'2424—dc22
2005001025

Printed and bound in the United States

10   9   8

Text design and layout by Virginia Scott Bowman

This book was typeset in Sabon with Michelangelo, Usherwood,
and Avenir as display typefaces

For my children

✳

CONTENTS

ACKNOWLEDGMENTS

Cabala,* from whence the tarot was derived, simply means "receive." The ancients used the word to indicate a uniquely personal experience that draws new or forgotten knowledge down from the heavens. The wise warned against revealing or teaching one's personal knowledge, fearing a great power could be unwittingly released.

In our time, a time of profound confusion and spiritual weakness, it is incumbent to share our knowledge on as wide a scale as possible. This book is an attempt to share but a few small kernels of wisdom from the Cabala.

I would like to thank my friends Dena and Shawna for their help and their encouragement throughout this project. I would also like to thank Vickie Trihy from Inner Traditions for her thoughtful questions and her exceptional ability to put all of this together in a way in which the reader can receive the teachings. In Talmudic times the teacher often had a *meturgeman,* one who would take the teacher's words and make them palatable to the public. Thank you, Meturgeman.

*Please see Note to the Reader on page x regarding the spelling of Cabala versus Kabbalah.

PREFACE

Out of Israel's 2,000-year exile a principle has emerged: From the deepest darkness comes the greatest light. For that reason, the cabalists say, we see out of the dark spot, the pupil of the eye.

Similarly, I discovered the tarot during the bleakest time of my life. Recently divorced after nineteen years of marriage, living alone without my children, I wandered the streets of New York City looking for something to engage my unwanted and newly secured freedom. My love of books drew me into a used bookstore, where I absently perused the volumes, wandering aimlessly from shelf to shelf without direction or inclination.

I do not know what drew me to that book about the tarot, but the word brought back a flood of memories. One Vermont winter night in the 1960s, my friend Laine had rolled in from California, straight from his little cabin on Happy Trails Road. He was filled to overflowing with his discovery of the tarot cards, and of Haile Selassie, Lion of Judah, Emperor of Ethiopia. (Rasta)

Soon after Laine's visit, I adopted a puppy and called her Jude. Jude and I hitchhiked to Maine. There we met a lumberjack who owned a 1952 Pontiac that, he insisted, once belonged to Haile Selassie, Emperor of Ethiopia. Charmed by the coincidence, I stayed and worked for him in exchange for shelter in a dilapidated farmhouse.

But to purchase the emperor's ex-car, which could have been mine for a mere $150, I would need to be resourceful. Because of my beard and long hair, employment in the local area was sketchy. So I journeyed to Bangor. By chance I encountered a rabbi who urged me to go to New York City and take up the study of Torah. Abandoning Haile Selassie, I traveled south. For the next two decades I dedicated myself to the study of the four levels of the Torah: the written word, the extrapolated idea, the metaphor, and the secret. For ten of those years I lived in Sfat, Israel, where some of the most influential cabalists lived and taught.

Twenty years after Laine's visit, I found myself staring at a large gilded book that promised to reveal "The Secret Knowledge of the tarot." One word stood out among all the other terms scattered through that book: Cabala. The author acknowledged that the true meaning of the tarot was locked up in the Cabala, but he had only a vague idea of its underlying principles. Drawings of the tarot cards appeared throughout his book; he identified them as belonging to the Rider-Waite deck.

I figured that if the cards were really cabalistic, I would be able to understand them on my own. Replacing the book on the shelf, I sought out my first tarot deck. What I discovered in that deck, and what I learned from many years of tarot study and practice, is the subject of this book.

The Talmud says that one's fifties are years of advising. Following this tradition, I took my little table and a few folding chairs, and went out on the road to become an itinerant teacher, teaching Torah by means of the tarot and advising the body through the voice of the spirit.

Note to the reader: Although the established convention as put forth by the rabbis has Kabbalah spelled with a *K*—the rabbinic kosher stamp—I prefer Cabala because it is more to the point. The Cabala is the most feminine of the Jewish teachings; even among the esoteric works, Cabala is the ultimate hidden secret. Therefore, in my opinion, Cabala should be written with a curve, denoting the feminine, and not defined by the line of the rabbis. Rigidity, the line, is the antithesis of the subtle, ephemeral truths that swim in the deep waters of the Cabala.

INTRODUCTION

ANCIENT ROOTS OF THE TAROT

The tarot cards are a vehicle of truth. These seventy-eight numbered and illustrated cards are believed to have their roots in the earliest Jewish spiritual tradition. The current cards have been used for over five hundred years, since the time of the Spanish Inquisition and the forced conversions of the Jewish people to Christianity. But the tarot's origins far predate modern history. I am convinced that tarot originated as a clandestine means for the captive tribes of Israel to study their sacred texts. The configuration of images and symbols embedded in the cards reflects the ancient esoteric knowledge known as Cabala. By exploring the historic roots and cabalistic elements of the tarot, we can derive the fullest and truest meaning from this ancient instrument.

The pictures on the cards are an outgrowth of the first captivity of the people of Israel in Egypt. There the children of Israel were slaves in a land where written language took the form of pictures—hieroglyphics. The experience of living in subjugation in Egypt and the subsequent exodus therefrom fused the twelve tribes into one people. It also indelibly engraved picture language upon the oral traditions and legends of the people.

Israel endured a second captivity a millennium after their liberation from Egypt, this time in Babylon, or Persia. Conquered by Nebuchadnezzar, their Temple destroyed and the people carried off

1

in chains, they lived as strangers in the land of their oppressors. Although they rose to positions of importance in the court of Persia, they remained a people apart. An official by the name of Haman, known as "the persecutor of the Jews," hatched a plot to destroy the entire people. Their fate depended upon chance—a game, the casting of lots to determine the date of the massacre. But the tables were turned by Esther, the Persian king's Jewish wife, who exposed the plot to her husband; Haman was put to death and the Jewish people were saved. (That miracle, celebrated in the holiday of Purim, which means "lottery" in the Persian language, is recounted in the book of Esther.) Encouraged by Cyrus the Great, Esther's son and the next king of Persia, the Jews returned to Jerusalem and began to recover their learning and to rebuild their Temple.

A few hundred years later Israel was invaded by Alexander the Great. His conquest had an immense impact on the Jewish people as witnessed by many references and tales in the sacred texts known as the Talmud. In one such tale, Alexander demanded that the rabbis lead him to paradise. The rabbis agreed, but when they reached the gates of paradise, an angel appeared to inform Alexander that he could not enter because he had killed. However, since he was a king, the angel gave Alexander a present, a consolation prize: a small round stone. The angel told him, "Nothing can outweigh this stone."

Sure enough, when Alexander returned from paradise, he found that no matter what was placed upon the pan opposite the little stone, it could not tip the scale. Alexander called in the rabbis and asked the meaning of this phenomenon. The rabbis explained that the round stone was an eyeball, and that the eye is never satisfied. As proof, the rabbis sprinkled some dust on the scale opposite from the little stone and tipped the pan. Only when one dies and the eye turns back to dust does the eye find satisfaction.

Alexander had big eyes. He wanted to conquer the world, but instead he died at thirty-three. In his dust was planted the Hellenization of Israel.

In those days Greek culture was centered on idolatry. The resistance of the Jewish people to idolatry brought edicts and cruel decrees from the Greek oppressors. Under the penalty of death, the study of Torah (the Jewish religion) was abolished. At this point, the tarot evolved—as a game of cards, a game of cat and mouse.

The Jewish people feigned idleness. They convinced their oppressors that without the Torah they had nothing to do. The idlers ostensibly took to gambling with cards, but this was really a clandestine form of study.

Once the Maccabees expelled the Greeks from Israel in 164 B.C.E. and Israel became, again, a Jewish kingdom, the tarot cards dropped from sight. Not long after that the Romans followed the Greeks. They despoiled the land of Israel and subjugated the Jewish nation; they burned the Holy Temple and exiled the people, scattering them to the four directions, dispersing them to every corner of the earth.

After Roman general Titus destroyed the Second Temple in 70 C.E., a group of rabbis succeeded in persuading the Romans to give them the city of Yavneh, where they presided for over two hundred years. There they wrote and assembled the Talmud. Composed in two sections, Mishnah and Gemara, the Talmud speaks in riddles and is rich in implication. Many archetypes employed in the tarot cards are drawn from the Talmud.

A thousand years after the Talmud was completed, the cards resurfaced—in response first to Jewish disputations with Catholic theologians, then to political and religious persecutions, and ultimately to the Inquisition. The tarot enabled those who would be true to the faith of Israel to study Torah without detection.

Reading the cards in these dangerous times had to be a game played as much through eye contact and the use of subtle gestures as by overt interpretation. The remnants of this interplay may still be found in the gesticulations and comic theater practiced in *yeshivas* (Jewish houses of learning) around the world.

CABALISTIC ELEMENTS
OF THE TAROT

Truth, אמת (*emet*) in Hebrew, is written with the first, middle, and last letters of the Hebrew alphabet (א *aleph,* מ *mem,* ת *tav*) to remind us that truth possesses a beginning, middle, and end.* The Torah, the inclusive name for the over-3,500-year-old tradition of the Jewish people, teaches the beginning, the end, and the purpose of all things. No wonder that the tarot, as a way to truth, arose out of Torah.

Truly understanding the tarot calls for a general grasp of the Torah as well as basic cabalistic principles. While the Torah has been open and available for all who wish to study it, both in Hebrew and in the many languages of the dispersion, the Cabala, or secret learning, has been concealed until relatively recently. This once-hidden knowledge surfaced only five hundred years ago in Sfat, northern Israel, through the teachings of Isaac Luria, the Ari, or Lion.

The Ari and his students unlocked the meaning of the book called the Zohar, or Brilliance. Written at the time of the destruction of the Second Temple in Jerusalem 2,000 years ago, the Zohar sealed the key to the secret learning inside its pages. Just as the Talmud is the book of the oral and wisdom tradition, so the Zohar is the book of the Cabala.

Two hundred years after the Ari's accomplishments, a Ukrainian rabbi known as the Baal Shem Tov founded Hasidism. A Hasid is one who has *hasidut*—"knowledge of the vessel that holds the light." The Cabala is that light. We are now in the tenth generation of the Hasidim who took the light of the Cabala and made its sophisticated concepts accessible to all people through their writings.

The Cabala teaches us to interpret the physical world through spiritual understanding. Drawing from cabalistic wisdom, tarot provides a clear language that can address the physical and the spiritual. I invite you, the reader, to tour the spirit realm in whose web we are meticulously embedded, through the vehicle of the deck of tarot cards.

---

*Hebrew words are written and read from right to left.

By the light of the Cabala, the tarot cards become legible. The cards and their configuration transform into a mirror; the diverse combinations of cards form a message, tell a story, reveal the process of the intricate interplay between the body and the soul.

I have read cards for many years, in numerous situations, venues, and circumstances. I have never seen a human life without purpose, or a darkness so bereft of hope that it could not lead to light. The tarot proclaims the holy individual, full of complexities from desire to love, from depression to victory. The human being, like each individual snowflake with a peculiar geometry never to be repeated, is unique. It is in our uniqueness that we are holy—each person a divine book in the celestial library of the Creator.

A NOTE ABOUT
GENDER IN THE CABALA

The precepts of Cabala are rooted in archetypal models of male and female. According to Cabala, humankind is a conduit between heaven and earth; the purpose of man, like a lightning bolt, is to bring the light down to earth and the purpose of woman is to take that light and grow something upon the earth. We are all a composite of male and female functioning in both realms, but the primordial distinction between man and woman—heaven and earth—and how that distinction is represented in our human form should never be overlooked or minimized in the pursuit of convention. Many of these ideas juxtapose man and woman in a way that may seem unfamiliar to modern minds; nonetheless, conventions change. The immutable inherent truth stamped on our flesh and carried in the pulse of our blood is a wisdom come from the bosom of the Creator.

SACRED PATTERNS
IN THE TAROT

The matrix of divisions and interrelationships among the cards that comprise the tarot mirror the divine "blueprint" of creation found in the Cabala. In this chapter we will look at how the sacred patterns and concepts of the Torah and the Cabala are embedded in the structure of the tarot.

THE LANGUAGE OF CREATION

Speech is a form of action; as the Torah says, "God spoke the world into being." Creation is a language—a language of rules of communication between Creator and creation known as the laws of nature. The Creator does not rely on omnipotence to interact with us, but rather always plays by the rules of creation. The Creator's great love for us fuels creation. Our Creator desires to be known to us, to live with us in this physical, moment-by-moment world that the Hasidim call *dira betouchtonnim,* a lowly dwelling place.

This desire on the part of the Creator is illustrated by the following parable.

Once there was a particular scandal that required a scapegoat, so they chose a poor man, and the governor gave permission for the unfortunate man to be hanged. Now this poor man had a friend, and when the friend heard what had happened, the friend presented himself before the governor while they stood at the gallows and confessed to the crime for which his friend was to be hanged.

The condemned man saw that his friend was offering to save his life by being hanged instead of him. He cried out, "I demand to be hanged!" and the two took to bickering over who should be hanged. The governor understood what was happening, called a halt to their wrangling, and said, "I will hang you both if you don't admit me to your friendship."

In the same way, through our love for one another, the Creator of the heavens and earth finds a dwelling place among us. It is through the soul that the Creator and the individual meld.

The tarot is a spiritual language that reveals the soul. In earthly life the Creator speaks to all of us through numbers and words that produce vision. The tarot draws its images and symbols from the visionary language of the Torah and the Cabala. Through understanding this language, one can begin to interpret not only the cards in the tarot deck but also the cards dealt to us through life.

The tarot cards do not speak with a harsh voice. The voice is always gentle and full of meaning. There is no right or wrong in the tarot; there is only the striving for a consistent message.

TORAH:
THE FOUNDATION

The word Torah comes from the word *mora*, or teaching. In the Torah, Creation is described as being a vast ocean of light. The Creator looked upon this light and from that reflection drew the pattern of Creation.

Thirty-five hundred years ago Moses, our teacher, climbed the mountain called Sinai, and there presented the Creator with two cubes of sapphire. According to scripture, the Creator engraved the two cubes with the 165 words of the Ten Commandments. Tradition also has it that at that same time, Moses received the 600,000 letters that would make up the Five Books of Moses.* These letters came in the form of the shards from the engraving of the Ten Commandments by "the finger of God." The Ten Commandments and the Five Books of Moses comprise the written Torah. The Torah was meant to simplify the celestial knowledge of Creation into a pattern accessible by the human being.

The pattern taught in the Torah and the pattern exhibited in the tarot are the same. Seeing pattern in creation is fundamental to recognizing one's individual purpose in life.

The Torah's primary purpose is to provide guidance in humanity's search for truth, not to declare "truths." The Torah is a vehicle for expressing complex reality: what is truly real and therefore is called by the name Torat Emet, or the Teachings of Truth. It was conceived as a coherent text able to stand up to meticulous examination and contemplation.

Maintaining the integrity of the Torah at the simplest level sets the standard for this pursuit of truth. A rule governs the study of the Torah: The simple meaning of the written Torah can never be tampered with. The simple meaning of the Torah is not always the literal sense of the words. For example, take the phrase "An eye for an eye; a tooth for a tooth." There was never an instance of a rabbi taking out someone's eye, God forbid, for that would contradict the Torah. Instead it was clearly understood that the phrase distinguished between the value of a tooth, which is one of thirty-two, and that of an eye, which is half of the whole. The commentary of

---

*The Five Books of Moses prophesy the history of the world from the creation of the first two human beings, Adam and Eve, until the twelve tribes of the Jewish people enter into the land of Israel forty years after the receiving of the Ten Commandments.

Rashi, Rabbi Shlomo Ben Yitchoki, has for a thousand years provided the standard for the simple explanation of the Torah.

Today, as in the earliest times, the Torah text is written by a highly dedicated scribe on a scroll made from the finely worked hide of a kosher animal. The standard of legibility for a Torah scroll is set by a child: If the child can read the letter, then it is a valid letter. Should even one letter in the Torah be missing or broken (the white of the parchment can be seen as a crack in the letter) or of doubtful construction, the entire Torah becomes invalid. That is how the integrity of the Torah is guarded and guaranteed.

In addition to the written Torah, there are three more levels of Torah knowledge, which are referred to collectively as the oral Torah: the Law, or Talmud; the Metaphor, or Midrash; and the Secret, or Zohar. This labyrinthine web of knowledge allowing for innumerable nonconflicting interpretations was transmitted orally for more than a thousand years. The oral tradition can be likened to the flesh upon the human skeleton—the law resides in the head, the story (metaphor) in the heart, and the secret between the legs. The flesh and form of the body change throughout one's life but the skeleton (the written Torah) always remains the same.

During the two thousand years of exile since the destruction of the Temple in Jerusalem, the oral Torah has been recorded in writing and continues to be enlarged with new interpretations. But those who would interpret the Torah in its written form composed more than three thousand years ago may not alter a single letter stroke or disturb the child's understanding. The oral tradition never detaches itself from the written word, but scrupulously maintains the integrity of the Torah. Not even in its most formal, esoteric attire can the simple meaning of the Torah be sacrificed to a more complex understanding. Therefore, baseless assertions will not be confused with valid conjecture. And so, even after more than a thousand years in the land of Israel and another two thousand years dispersed throughout the world, every Torah scroll anywhere in the world contains exactly the same text, written by hand with quill and ink.

CABALA:
THE FRAMEWORK

By contrast with the Torah, the tarot cards do not have the same validity and exactness. The tarot has gone through numerous transformations over the last few thousand years as it was transported from country to country and adapted to different cultures. Nonetheless, the tarot has retained its basic structure, which is derived from the Cabala, the key to the Torah's mystical secret meaning. The four card suits, the attributes of the number and court cards in the Minor Arcana, and the number and character of the cards in the Major Arcana all have their source in the teachings of the Cabala.

The complexity of the Torah can always be reduced down to four: the four-letter name of the Creator, the four worlds, the four elements, and the four levels of Torah. The Creator's Name, the original Name from which all names stem, has four letters: the male letter Yud, followed by the female letter Hey, the male Vav, and ending with a second Hey (יהוה YHVH). When placed vertically, they represent the four spirit worlds. In the tarot the four spirit worlds are represented through the four elements—fire, wind, water, and earth—which in turn are represented by the four suits.

The Ari taught that the key to the Cabala—to the knowledge of the physical and the spiritual realms—is expressed in our physical being. The remainder of this chapter will focus on the cabalistic principles encoded in the human form, and how they in turn shape the tarot.

The Four Spirit Worlds

There are four spirit worlds imprinted in our being, encompassing all of human experience from our lowest impulses to our noblest aspirations. These worlds are not outside of us but rather within all things of creation.

The four spiritual worlds—Atzilut (the World of Emanation), Briah (the World of Creation), Yetzirah (the World of Formation),

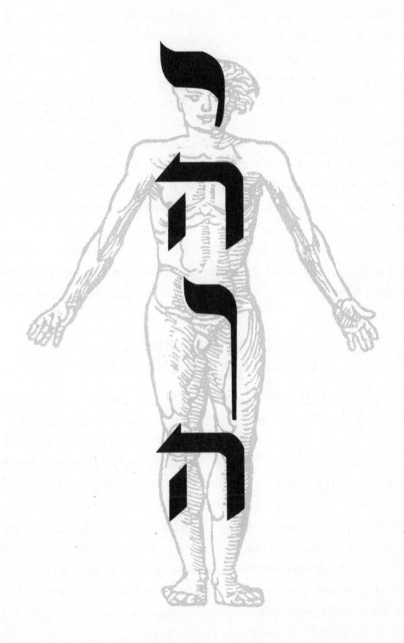

The Name of the Creator (Yud-Hey-Vav-Hey)

and Asiyah (the World of Action)—are the source of life for the human, the animal, the plant, and the earth. There is nothing in creation that does not have a spiritual component. A primary difference between the physical and the spiritual is that in the physical domain all things are eroding, decaying, evaporating, or dying, whereas in the spirit world nothing dies.

The four spirit worlds and the physical world are distinguished by the amount of divine light that filters through them. The highest of the four spirit worlds is called Atzilut, from a word meaning "close," because it is the closest world to the infinite light of the Creator, the light of infinite potential. It is representative of the soul. The highest world of Atzilut can be compared to the human soul that funnels life to the body.

The next three worlds, Briah, Yetzirah, and Asiyah, are associated with our earthly life, and the ego that recognizes the difference between Creator and creation. We will come back to them shortly.

DIVINE PATTERNS:
THE MATRIX OF THE TAROT

The tarot deck is divided into the Major Arcana, consisting of twenty-two cards, and the Minor *arcana,* of fifty-six cards, for a total of seventy-eight cards. (The word arcana derives from the word *arcane,* or "secret.") Three obvious cabalistic patterns can be discerned in these sets of cards. First, the twenty-two cards of the Major Arcana correspond with the twenty-two letters of the Hebrew alphabet. Second, within the Minor Arcana are four suits, or decks, which correspond with the four spirit worlds and the related four elements. Third, each suit has fourteen cards. The number fourteen correlates to the ten parts of the body known as the Sefirot and the five parts of the soul. (That there are fourteen and not fifteen cards will be explained.) In the pages that follow, we will explore the significance of each of these patterns in the tarot.

The Suits and the Four Spirit Worlds

In the Cabala, each of the four elements corresponds to one of the four spirit worlds. The four suits of the Minor Arcana cards embody this association.

In the suits of the Minor Arcana, these four spiritual worlds are expressed through ancient archetypes of the four elements, as follows:

> *the staff*—fire
> *the sword*—air
> *the cup*—water
> *the coin*—earth

For example, the first spirit world, Atzilut, is a world of fire. In this world, the essence of life, the male and the female, is at one with the Creator. This is the world of the soul. It is this fire of life that never dies, but recedes back to its source at the end of life. Fire indicates the future, for light illuminates what is before us. In the tarot, the Staff is the symbol of fire.

Briah, the world of thought, is exemplified by the element air, the invisible. Thinking is the closest we come to conscious spiritual experience. Like the air, our thoughts cannot be seen and possess little weight but they are inexorably there. The Sword, because it cuts through the air, is a symbol of the invisible and represents air in the tarot.

Yetzirah, the world of emotions, is associated with the element water. The nature of liquid is to spread unless it is constrained. Emotions tend to overflow their vessel or, when dammed up, become a considerable force. The Cup represents this element in the tarot.

Asiyah, the world of action, is symbolized by the coin, or Pentacle, as it is called in the Rider-Waite deck (source of the card illustrations used in this book) and others. It takes a lot of soul/fire, thoughts/air, emotions/water to forge the coin. Similarly, it takes all our capacity to make our mark in the physical world.

SUIT / SYMBOL CORRESPONDENCES		
SPIRIT WORLD	ELEMENT	SUIT SYMBOL
Atzilut/Soul	Fire	Staff
Briah/Thought	Air	Sword
Yetzirah/Emotions	Water	Cup
Asiyah/Action	Earth	Pentacle

Each element is a metaphor. Fire reaches up but it must be rooted to the physical in order to exist. Air is calm, ethereal, and easily disturbed. Water reaches down and always finds its way to the sea, and earth is strong and immutable. By understanding the characteristics and nature of the four elements and their innate connections to the four spirit worlds, we can begin to decipher the secrets hidden within the tarot.

The Numbered Cards and the Ten Sefirot

In addition to representing the cabalistic notion of the four worlds in the form of the four suits, the tarot further separates each of the four suits into two sections: one of nine cards (Two through Ten), representing the body, and one of five cards (the royal cards: Page, Knight, Queen, King, and Ace), representing the soul. The nine numbered cards plus the set of royal cards mirror the cabalistic construct known as the Ten Sefirot. Each numbered card's meaning derives in part from the attributes of its corresponding Sefira. The number one is missing because it is replaced with the five court cards, which relate to the five parts of the soul. The merging of soul into body takes place in the first Sefira, as will be explained.

The word Sefirot is derived from the phrase *eben saphir*, or sapphire stone, and indeed one can think of the Sefirot as ten stones of different luminosity that reflect the white light of the Creator. Each Sefira governs a particular aspect of human experience. The Ten Sefirot are grouped in three categories corresponding to the three lower spirit worlds—the intellect, the emotions, and action.

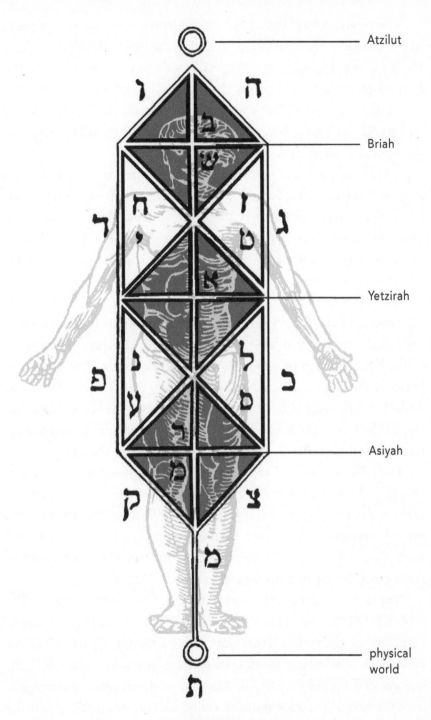

The four worlds

The first three Sefirot—Chochma, Binah, and Daat—are aspects of the intellect. The intellect is housed in the brain, which is made in the form of a triangle—two frontal lobes and the cerebellum at the back of the head. The brain is the physical vessel for the light emanating from the soul. The Cabala holds that the soul is very large, and starlike in appearance. Only a small beam of its light enters into the human brain to initiate life.

Chochma translates as "wisdom" but is often explained as "the Power of What." This nomenclature describes the brain's experience of inspiration—receiving a flash of the spiritual light of the soul. Once we receive this flash, and we ask the question "What is this?" the answer is within reach—the information has already entered in. Chochma corresponds to the right lobe of the brain.

Binah is related to the word for "builder." It means "understanding" and refers to the left side of the brain. In Cabala these two lobes are called "mother and father never separated," as these two regions of the brain, though of opposite nature, work as one. The difference between the right and left sides of the brain is as clear as light and darkness. The right side of the brain sees the light, but it is the left side of the brain, the feminine side, that takes the light of inspiration into the darkness and develops it to form a salient thought.

Daat, or "knowing," represents that spark of sudden realization, though only momentary, that is the final goal of intellect—to actually make a decision because you just *know*. It corresponds to the third eye, or cerebellum. Binah and Daat are represented by the numbered cards Two and Three. (There is no card number One—Chochma is represented by the five royal cards, as we will see shortly.)

The next group of Sefirot are representative of the emotions. The six Sefirot of the emotions correspond with the six days of Creation. Each day of Creation corresponds to a particular aspect of human experience or what the Torah considers emotions. For example, light was created on the first day of Creation and this event corresponds with the first of the six emotions, called *chesed,* or kindness. It is the attribute of giving freely and completely.

Though the translations of the names of these six Sefirot do not sound like emotions to those used to thinking in terms of sad and happy, by looking deeper into this concept we discover they are the mirror to all human experience. The first of the Sefirot of emotions, Chesed—Kindness, indicates an endless capacity for the human being to give; it is the mother's milk of creation. The second Sefira, Gevurah—Severity, is an infinite capacity to hold back, restrain, and even eradicate. All strength derives from this attribute. The third Sefira, Tiferet—Beauty, is a combination of the previous two Sefirot. A melding of the kind and the severe is what produces beauty—the beauty of truth that arises from balancing opposites. The fourth Sefira is Netzach—Victory, the quality of persistence. Its opposite is the fifth Sefira, Hod—Splendor. This is the Sefira of patience and hidden strength. The sixth Sefira of emotion, Yesod—Foundation, aligns beneath Beauty/Truth. This is the Sefira of sexuality and creativity. These six attributes are depicted in the tarot cards numbered Four to Nine.

The three Sefirot of the intellect fall within the realm of the spirit world Briah/Thought, and the six Sefirot of the emotions reflect the spirit world of Yetzirah/Emotions. The lowest spirit world, Asiyah/Action, corresponds with the tenth Sefira—Malchut, or Speech. This Sefira is represented by the Ten in the numbered cards.

Malchut/Speech is also called Kingship, because it is through the word that the king rules. Speech, more than any other human quality, separates us from the animals. The animal, at best, can utter guttural sounds meant to convey its will. The animal can growl or purr or shriek or bark, but it cannot express a complex thought.

Thoughts suffuse our emotions, generating a vibration that rides upon the breath, resounds in the throat, breaks across the teeth, and finally passes through the lips—words projected into the world. Our will, generated by the goal of pleasure, is filtered through our mental senses, elaborated in our emotions, and finally spoken into the world. This progression can be seen in the illustration of the Tree

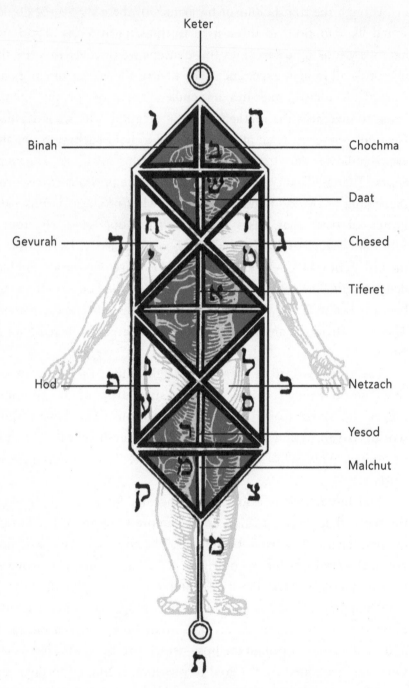

The Tree of Life
The Ten Sefirot superimposed on the human form

of Life on page 18, moving from the head downward through the Ten Sefirot. The tarot cards reflect this same progression.

In Cabala, speech is metaphorically equated with giving birth to action. Thus, our unique ability to articulate thoughts into speech, which is considered action, represents the divine woman in each of us.

The Royal Cards and the Five Parts of the Soul

As we have seen, the first ten cards of each suit represent the six emotions and speech (numbers Four to Ten) and their convergence with the intellect (numbers Two and Three). In lieu of a card number One, the first Sefira, Chochma, is represented by the five royal cards—the five parts of the soul as it manifests in the body. The soul enters into the body through the right side of the brain as an infinitesimal ray of spiritual light. In the Cabala, the soul is seen as having five distinct parts.

In the soul itself is body and soul. The lower three parts of the soul correspond to the body—the legs/Action; the upper body/ Emotions; the head/Intellect—and the soul of the soul is divided into two parts that are really one: Will and Pleasure.

The Major Arcana and the Twenty-two Hebrew Letters

Just as the suits in the Minor Arcana represent the four elements, the twenty-two cards of the Major Arcana represent the fifth element— the pure, unique soul—starlike in dimension, connected to the body through a thread of light. The human being is both male and female, so the essence of the human, the soul in its most pristine state, is also male and female. The Cabala describes this dual essence as Will and Pleasure. From Pleasure, the innermost power, woman emerges; from Will, the outer expression of the essence, comes man.

The twenty-two letters of the Hebrew language represent each of the male and female aspects of the Ten Sefirot plus the two essences,

Will and Pleasure. The twenty-two cards of the Major Arcana represent these twenty-two letters and thus express the male and female sides of our nature. These twenty-two letters and the Sefira qualities that they represent are embedded within each human soul. The Major Arcana are numbered from zero to twenty-one and these numbers reflect the duality of each of the Ten Sefirot, yielding an intricate portrait of human experience.

FREEDOM AND INTENTION IN THE TAROT

Freedom of choice, according to that great repository of wisdom, the Talmud, is found through one's intention. The mind exercises freedom of choice by considering the reasons for one's actions; the heart expresses freedom of choice through the emotions of love and fear. Through the collaboration of head and heart, the distillation of the soul's intentions struggles through the physical body, labors, then gives birth to an action.

Freedom of choice exists only in this physical realm. In the spirit worlds the light of creation is too powerful and obvious to allow one to go against the will of the Creator. Only here, in this dark world, shielded from the divine light, are we able to choose between good and bad. This freedom of choice must never be tampered with by making a prediction when using a spiritual medium like the tarot.

When doing a tarot reading, it is important for the reader to understand that the tarot is a spiritual language meant to transmit a message from the soul. The person whose cards are being read is particularly sensitive and vulnerable at the time of the reading. It is essential that the reader not restrict a person's free will through his or her words. Predicting the future is a blatant disrespect of the delicate human spirit, and defies the underlying purpose of the tarot—which is to help us clarify intention, not impose it.

THE TWENTY-TWO SECRETS

In this chapter we will examine the twenty-two cards of the Major Arcana not through a microscope, but through the telescope of creation. Using the Ten Sefirot as our guide through the worlds of creation we begin to see a pattern emerging and structure taking hold. We know that in Cabala the human being can be broken down into seven body parts plus three divisions of intellect divided between the two lobes and the cerebellum—ten parts in all. We live in a world that is a mirror of our human form: a world of seven landmasses with three oceans. The solar system we dwell in has ten worlds with corresponding attributes to the Ten Sefirot. This pattern of ten is also evident in the tarot cards.

Truth is the composite of the parts; to see a thing in its whole is to see the truth. The cards, like the Sefirot, do not have precise meanings but they do have attributes, like a palette of ten colors that can be blended in an infinite number of ways.

In the Cabala, Will and Pleasure are the two essences of creation. Essence is defined as that which cannot be seen. Will is the essence of man and Pleasure the essence of woman. Each essence has ten lights emanating from it—the Ten Sefirot. In the Cabala, light is used as a metaphor for spiritual illumination. Just as physical light has the ability to behave like both a particle and a wave, so too spiritual light is the manifestation of two opposites: the innate male and female mirrored within the ten luminaries—the Ten Sefirot.

These essences are made visible in the form of the Hebrew alphabet. Each essence, illuminated in ten unique ways, was formed by the Creator into letters. Thus, the twenty-two letters that form the basis of the Hebrew language are equally divided between male and female: the Will (masculine) and his ten lights and Pleasure (female) and her ten lights. This is how the Hebrew language, through form and number, embodies the whole of creation.

The relationship of Will and Pleasure and their sets of ten lights to the twenty-two letters of the Hebrew alphabet resembles that between the twenty-two amino acids that form the gene and the twenty-two pairs of chromosomes that make up our cells. (The twenty-third pair determines sex and could be considered like the vowels beneath the Hebrew letters that govern pronunciation.) The Cabala teaches that creation is a combination of linked letters in an infinite array of intersecting possibilities in much the same way that the genes and chromosomes through their interlocking combinations govern the characteristics of the person. Tarot cards, particularly the twenty-two cards of the Major Arcana, are vehicles of these esoteric secrets.

THE DESIGN

The Ten Sefirot from which we derive the cabalistic interpretation of tarot are connected to specific regions of the human body. The design of the body is neither random nor purely a result of biological programming, but rather intentional. It is a picture, full of wisdom, drawn by our Maker. The human body can be drawn as three triangles stacked upright. The two hemispheres of the brain and the third eye make the triangle of the intellect and the six emotions form the two triangles of emotion. Thought and emotion produce speech;

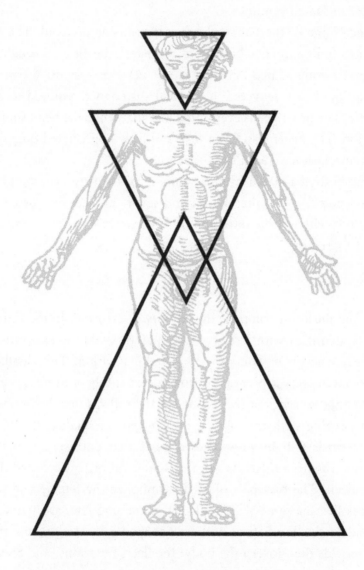

This representation conveys how light comes in from the heavens, enters the head, passes down through the spine and the six emotions, and exits through speech or action.

speech, the tenth attribute *(Sefirot)*, is likened to a woman giving birth. (The configuration of the two lower triangles is the origin of the Star of David symbol.)

The Name of the Creator is engraved inside the soul. The soul conducts light into the brain and animates the flesh through the immensely complicated circuitry of our nervous system. Warm and pulsing, the heart delivers the physical sustenance required to support life. The heart keeps everything moving, while the head supplies direction. The heart also has a rare and little appreciated quality: It can connect directly with the Creator.

The body, animated by the pumping heart, traverses the physical environment to realize action and satisfy choice. Exercising our freedom to choose, the intention of the heart, we come face-to-face with the Creator.

Light and darkness comprise the entirety of creation. In the Cabala, male is identified with light because male sexuality is external and revealed, whereas a woman's sex is hidden within. This duality is played out in every aspect of creation. Either subtly or overtly, each of the twenty-two cards of the Major Arcana reflects this dichotomy.

In keeping with this underlying concept of duality, the Major Arcana cards will be presented in pairs that correspond to their cabalistic themes rather than in the numerical order accorded them in the deck. The first pair of cards symbolize the female and male essences Pleasure and Will, while the remaining ten card pairs correspond to the Ten Sefirot and are grouped according to the three spirit worlds that govern the body: Intellect, Emotions, and Speech/ Action.

PLEASURE AND WILL

Pleasure is seen in Cabala as the essence of woman, and is designated by the circle. The circle receives. It is always bounded and complete. Will, the essence of man, is designated by the line. Will—the line—is the outer manifestation of essence, while Pleasure—the circle—is the hidden, undefined, formless energy contained within all things. Circles can always be made bigger, while lines can only be made longer. The circle is the place of creation. The line is the thread of light that illuminates space.

THE HANGED MAN.

THE TOWER.

✒ THE HANGED MAN, THE TOWER

The Hanged Man card depicts a young man hung upside down by his foot. A yellow crown, representing pleasure, encircles his head. The crown, *keter*, is the cabalistic symbol for pleasure, that source of all our energy and reason for all action. The all-encompassing motivation of pleasure is seen in Cabala as being beyond logic, and is therefore sometimes also called chaos. In this card image we see that just beyond the intellect, pleasure—the fountain of life—overflows in a fuming state of unbridled energy.

The Hanged Man's heart is elevated above his head. In the human body the heart is beyond logic; when the heart is elevated above the head, it is a sign that chaos rules. Cabalistically, chaos is what precedes logic and is considered one of the higher realms. The realm of logic is further from the singularity of the Light Without End; it is the chaos of light and darkness, Pleasure and Will, that connects the infinite with the finite.

The line—the essence of male—is represented in the tarot cards by The Tower, that most phallic of images. Here a bolt of lightning strikes The Tower and blows off its crown in a burst of fire as men jump from the window. Will is single-minded: Everything else can jump out of the window. Nothing stands before Will.

INTELLECT

The Zohar teaches that Torah can be understood as seventy different faces, with seventy different perspectives of truth. The Torah often speaks in terms of the seventy nations of the world and their seventy tongues. The Jewish judges in the time of the Temple had to be proficient in all seventy languages before they could sit on the court. These seventy faces abide in each and every letter of the Torah, and everyone who takes from the Torah finds many faces that explain the same thing in many ways.

With so many different faces to knowing, how do we really *know* something? The place in the body for knowing is the third eye. The third eye is not a tangible part of the body, but rather a state of

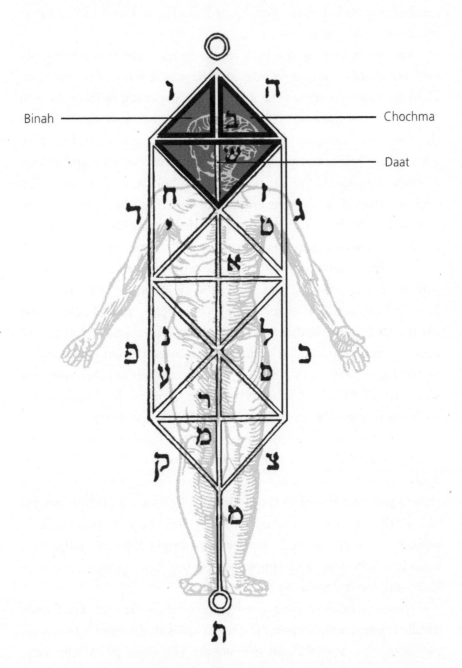

Binah — Chochma

Daat

The upper three lights

advanced consciousness. Tradition locates the third eye opposite the cerebellum, buried deep within our reptilian self and hinted at on the empty space of the forehead.

The cerebellum, at the back of the head, is concerned primarily with the coordination of muscles and the maintenance of equilibrium. Here the brain reconciles the information streaming in from the two hemispheres of the brain. The result is projected upon the middle of the forehead, initiating an unusual, temporal experience: The third eye emerges just long enough to elicit an electric impulse and deliver a momentary spark. Similar to a lightning bolt emitted between two opposite charges, such is the experience within our brain between the seeing of the right side of the brain and the hearing in the left. Where there is conclusion and consensus there is illumination.

The upper three lights form a triangle of intellectual illumination: Chochma, Binah, and Daat, the right brain, the left brain, and the third eye. The two hemispheres of the brain, Chochma and Binah, act in unison; this is termed by the Cabala as "Mother and Father never separated." This unison produces a visual and auditory rendering of the soul's longing. The cerebellum synchronizes the sound to the form and projects a picture upon the forehead, as if it were the screen of a drive-in theater. This is the impulse.

When the three lobes of the brain agree, the mind short-circuits and the fused light of the mind explodes in a flash. A spark from this flash enters into the spine and moves through the six emotions (Kindness, Severity, Beauty/Truth, Victory, Splendor, and Foundation), like a ball in a pinball machine bouncing from point to point accompanied by gongs and bells, buzzers and bright lights. Finally, after countless rebounds and flipper shots, the ball disappears into a hole—the mouth opens to emit speech.

The three lobes of the brain are mirrored on the face. The Zohar dwells at great length upon "the seven holes in the head": two eyes, two ears, two nostrils, and the mouth. The three pairs—the eyes, ears, and nostrils—correspond to the three lobes of the brain. The power to see resides in the right side of the brain while the power to hear is on the left. Knowing is in the center—smell ignites memory, which revisits the experience of knowing.

These three pairs are represented in the tarot deck's Major Arcana as The Emperor and The Empress, The Hermit and The High Priestess, and The Hierophant and Justice.

THE EMPEROR, THE EMPRESS

The right side of the brain is represented by The Emperor and The Empress. On both cards, an imperial figure sits on a throne—a man and a woman, each with a crowned head. The right side of the brain conducts, through a thin line of light, the soul's directives. Through what is called in Hebrew *chochma*, or the Power of What, the spirit world enters the physical in a burst of energy that the right side of the brain perceives as a question: *What?*

The Power of What is the power to awaken and be

conscious. The What sees everything but has no words to describes what is seen. The What is the smallest point of the lightning rod that the bolt of lightning seeks. It is through the smallness and humility of the What—and not by retraining the light through the ego of our intellect—that the soul is allowed entry into the body. Moses, our teacher, who received the Torah through his attribute of Humility, is often quoted in vexing times as saying *Mah anucnu,* or "What are we?"

The brain perceives the light from the soul as a palette of swirling colors. This primal blend in vivid hues is compressed into a snapshot of the soul's communication. The right side of the brain receives this communication. The Imperial pair, The Emperor and The Empress, send this message to the left side of the brain to be processed and understood. The Emperor represents the vision of the soul—he sees what is apparent; while the Empress represents the inner vision—she reads between the lines. We can think of The Emperor as embodying sight, and The Empress as insight.

THE HERMIT, THE HIGH PRIESTESS

The Hermit and The High Priestess correspond to the left side of the brain. Where the right side of the brain is drenched in light, the left side of the brain is dark and full of sound. A similar correspondence between sight and insight is mirrored in the left side of the brain: The Hermit hears that which is apparent; The High Priestess listens to what is beyond the simple meaning of the words.

The Hermit is the messenger who contracts the light of inspiration from the right side of the brain and

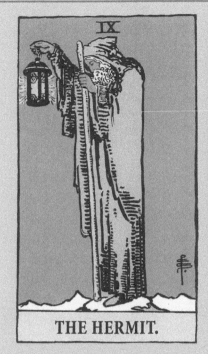

THE HERMIT.

THE HIGH PRIESTESS.

fits it into a lantern with which he journeys forth into the unknown. The capacity to restrain inspiration can be compared to holding one's tongue instead of speaking one's truth—it is the small light that informs the darkness, not the torch that blinds. This is male energy subservient to the female. In order to enter into the female, man must reduce himself like the sperm, which is the smallest cell of the body. It is interesting to note that in Jewish law, man is commanded to pleasure woman, to make his desires second to hers; it is in this way that woman can receive man.

The High Priestess sits on a throne in front of two flanking rows of pillars. The forward-most pillar of each row is inscribed with a letter. Transcribed into Hebrew, the two letters, b (ב—*bet*) and j (י—*yud*), have the numerical value twelve. The twelve pillars around the throne of The Priestess represent the zodiac.

THE HIEROPHANT.

JUSTICE.

The High Priestess sets her foot on the crescent moon. The orb of the world balances upon her head, the sign of chaos lies against her heart, and a scroll with the letters TORA rests on her lap. She is called the mother of children. She epitomizes understanding. She reigns over the light of inspiration drawn from the right side of the brain. When she has completed her task, she gives birth to knowing.

THE HIEROPHANT, JUSTICE

The Hierophant and Justice cards refer to the third eye and the Sefira of Daat. They represent a particular kind of knowing; knowing is implicit in judging. Both The Hierophant and Justice have a similar picture: Two commanding figures hold the symbol of their authority, one in the right hand (Justice) and the other (The

Hierophant) in the left. The keys at The Hierophant's feet depict hidden knowledge that resides in all of us. This is spiritual knowledge conferred to us from the heavens.

The authority of Justice is more physical, able to be weighed out, as depicted by the scale he holds in his left hand. He also takes his power from the spiritual, as shown through the sword, which, besides wheeling through the invisible air, dictates power in the physical world through the sharp edge of the blade.

In this physical world, disputes are settled by weighing the facts to determine what is true. Justice is charged with knowing the difference between the true and the false—logic determines what we believe is right. In the spiritual realm, our sense of justice is automatic. It comes like a flash of enlightenment—an epiphany.

The Hierophant portrays heavenly judgment. This is different from what we practice in this world because in heaven our thoughts are yells that all the heavens hear—all things testify to the truth. Justice, on the other hand, delivers the decision after weighing the facts. He is not infallible, but he is judge because he possesses the ability to distinguish between true and false.

EMOTIONS

The six emotions (Chesed—Kindness, Gevurah—Severity, Tiferet—Beauty/Truth, Netzach—Victory, Hod—Splendor, and Yesod—Foundation) are called Little Faces by the cabalists. The power of Will they call Big Faces. This nomenclature denotes that the Will is diffused through the brain and reemerges in the body as emotions. The emotions descend into the lower part of the body to give birth to action.

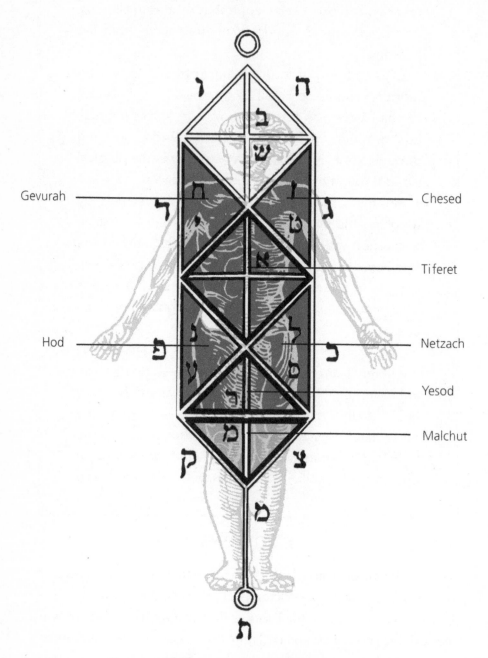

The six emotions and speech

Kindness

The lungs constrain the fire of the blood. The lungs tame the heart. That is why when we become upset, the first advice is to concentrate on breathing. The lungs bring wisdom to the troubled chaos of the emotions. The lungs are called Chesed, Kindness.

The lungs are represented as The Sun and The Star, the cards associated with the right arm. The right arm wields the kind hand.

THE SUN.

THE STAR.

↜ THE SUN, THE STAR

In The Sun card, the cycle is beginning: A very young child is riding atop a white horse as the sun is rising, flooding the land with light. In Cabala the concept of light is used as a metaphor for spiritual suste-nance because light, more than any other physical phenomenon, has the properties of kindness, warming and illuminating everything in it path. Light renews. A new beginning is signified by the child and by the horse, symbol of emotions, prancing with optimism before the rising sun.

The Star is brilliant but very far away. Its light passes through the naked woman, who transmutes the light into water, which she pours in plenitude from her vessels. Starlight, though appearing small and easily obliterated by the daylight or night clouds, is in actuality a much greater light than the illumination emanating from the sun. In life there is kindness that is apparent, warming us with the promise of renewal, but there is also a kindness that appears like a jewel with a delicate light that can enter into the depths of our being to change the course of our life if we dare to peer into the vast unknown.

Severity

The heart, which pumps blood into the body, is the paradigm of strength. It is represented in the tarot by the Death and Judgement cards.

DEATH, JUDGEMENT

Death rides a white horse and everyone bows down before it. Death is not just the ending; it is also the beginning, part of a cycle. The cycle seems to laugh at us everywhere we turn. Every celestial body in the solar system cycles around the sun. Seasons cycle. Woman cycles. Life cycles: From birth to death is half

DEATH.

JUDGEMENT.

the cycle. The magic of the heart resides in its ability to control the cycle—to stop the flow of blood to allow sufficient pressure to build before releasing it and letting a new cycle begin. The heart, which is the bastion of life, is also the repository of the past.

After each of the first five days of the Creation the Creator said, "Tov/good!" After the sixth and final day of Creation the Creator said, "Tov maod/very good." So the rabbis understood that finality is "very good." It is the ultimate end of the cycle that inspires life; knowing that death looms before us impels us to push ourselves beyond our limits. The power of Death is equal to the power of life: Each is, like night and day, an essential part of the whole.

In the Judgement card, coffins float on the water

and the naked dead rise to be reborn. The sound of the horn from the mouth of the angel Gabriel announces the decision from the heavenly court. Spiritual judgment and celestial justice are the end of the death process; now we can rise from the ashes and begin anew. As it says in the Sefer Yetzira, written 3,800 years ago by Avraham, father of the Jewish and Arab people, "All beginnings are rooted in their end and all endings rooted in their beginning."

Beauty/Truth

Truth is not what we think; truth is what we feel—an inexplicable emotion in our chest. The heart and the lungs together speak truth. It is fitting that we often trust our emotions over our brain, because the center of the heart, meaning in Cabala the intersection of lungs and heart, connects directly to the Creator.

From the center of the heart, we go beyond all restraints and boundaries. Both The Fool and The Magician represent the innate human ability to connect directly with the Creator. With a faithful heart, we may stand at the edge of the abyss; from the abyss we are able to wield our magic.

➤ THE MAGICIAN, THE FOOL

The Magician stands under a lush canopy, behind a table bearing the four elements. The cabalistic meanings embedded in this card are numerous. The canopy symbolizes the ability to bring the spiritual down to the physical, which is why Jewish marriages are performed beneath the chuppah. This idea of connecting heaven

THE MAGICIAN.

THE FOOL.

and earth is further expanded by the scepter pointing up in The Magician's right hand while the finger of the left hand points down. The four elements spread on the table before him signify that The Magician mixes elements according to the wisdom of the heart to produce the miraculous. Because everything is revealed, this is a male card.

The Fool, on the other hand, is about to walk off a cliff. He does not know how he will survive, but he knows he will because he walks with God. The Fool sees what even the wise cannot see. The dog at his side barks for The Fool to stop, but The Fool is carefree and holds a flower in his hand. In his satchel are also the four elements, but they are hidden because his magic is a deeper magic that cannot be revealed. The light that shines down upon him is pure white unadulterated light because The Fool's faith draws the Creator's notice. His faith is his magic.

Faith, אמנה *(emunah)* in Hebrew, shares its root אמן with אומן *(oman)*, the word for craftsman. An artisan does not have to think about where his hands go—he has perfectly trained limbs to do his work. Similarly, the skill of the heart is recognizing Truth. The faithful heart has an immediate, positive response to Truth.

Victory

The liver and the two kidneys purify the blood and add nutrients reduced down from the food and liquid the body consumes. The liver and the kidneys govern the lower extremities, the legs, in much the same way that the heart and lungs govern the arms. The legs comprise about half of the body's length. They connect us to the ground and enable us to stand, to run, and to dance. The head has intellect, the torso has emotions, the hips have drive. Drive does not come from reason; it has an energy that surpasses even passion. The legs will not allow for defeat, as demonstrated by the saying in boxing, "the last one standing."

The right leg is traditionally associated with *Netzach*, Victory, symbolized by The Chariot and Strength cards.

➤ THE CHARIOT, STRENGTH

In The Chariot card, a strong man in military garb is riding a chariot drawn by two Sphinxlike lions. This card represents male, external strength whose purpose is to quell the enemy. To harness the power of the wild

THE CHARIOT.

STRENGTH.

beast that lies within us all produces a formidable challenge to those who would oppose us.

Strength is pictured as a woman closing the mouth of a lion, not through physical exertion but with the female energy of inner strength as attested to by the infinity symbol above her head. There is an inner strength within us all, drawn from the infinite spirit world from where we came. It can calm turmoil with a smile and make the most hardened heart bow before it.

Splendor

While the right leg is pursuing victory, the left is prepared for retreat. This is the dance that balances us on the earth.

TEMPERANCE.

THE MOON.

➤ **TEMPERANCE, THE MOON**

The left leg is tied to the Sefira Hod, represented in the tarot by Temperance and The Moon. Temperance is woman at her most modest and demure. The sun is going down, and an angelic woman dips her foot into the water. Temperance is perhaps the gentlest of the cards. The energy of this card is quickly rebuffed by harshness. The quality of this card is patience, enduring and creative.

In The Moon card, the moon covers the sun.

Animals creep from the water. The separation of regenerative force from the river of life and the howling at the moon is indicative of the menstrual metaphor. With the dissolution of the lining of the uterus, the egg that had the potential to become a child if impregnated gets flushed from the body. The body lets go of its aspirations for that egg, thus making room for a new egg and a new opportunity

The ability to let go is the key to creativity. Creativity is a delicate light that comes out of the darkness. Through making ourselves small, by stepping back and letting go, creativity flourishes.

To go within and let it be is also a powerful tool during the turmoil of life. The symbolic meaning of menstruation is to divest ourselves of our effort and failures, to move on like a woman who has been trying to become pregnant.

Foundation

From where did male and female derive? What does gender mean? The combining of male and female, the commingling of opposite energies, the conjugational union that initiates life is among the greatest of mysteries. In Hebrew, the place in the human body that distinguishes male from female is called yesod which means foundation.

The two poles of sexuality, male and female, vie for dominance in the body. Sexuality is like light, which behaves at the same time like a wave and like a particle, dancer and dance occupying the same space. The marriage of wave and ray, of line and circle, produces a fluctuating dynamic, a spiral. The union of man and woman produces a child.

Sexuality pervades and brings forth the essence of all things:

Will and Pleasure, giving and receiving. The male and female sides of sexuality contain the duality of all things.

Sexual energy, more so than all the other energies in the body, is patently for another person. Pleasure and Will are intrinsic to sexuality. Sexuality tests our will and our intention. Sexual energy by itself has no morality: Flesh loves flesh. It is logic and love that give sense to our sexual actions.

Sexuality is represented in the Major Arcana as The Lovers and The Devil. These two cards resemble each other both in layout and in the figures represented on them, but they are the agents of entirely opposite intentions.

THE LOVERS.   THE DEVIL.

➤ THE LOVERS, THE DEVIL

On The Lovers card, an angel presides from the heavens over a naked man and woman modestly cavorting amid the luscious landscape. The nature of the human being is to do what is good and healthy for us; our natural inclination is to choose life. Nonetheless, we are seduced into that which is harmful. What advice is older than the warning against being carried away by our eyes, lest we become helpless as the heart swoons and confuses sexual appetite with happiness?

On The Devil card, the naked man and woman are in chains; between them The Devil holds fire that points down, in opposition to the nature of fire. The Devil card should be called שׂטָן (satan), a Hebrew word for the opposing force devised by the Creator to test creation. Without Satan there would be no free will—there would be nothing to choose against. Devil and Hell are not Jewish concepts; all physical creation returns back to the spiritual world at the end of the life cycle. But while on earth, Satan, or the Opposer, tries to subvert the good deed and pervert what is natural.

The Lovers are blessed; the light of creation beams down upon them, the heavens smile. They are unencumbered. By contrast, The Devil card has the male and female energies restrained; one might conjure up in this card the opposite of blessing, but it is not so. The Devil card should not be taken as a bad sign—there are no bad energies or unfavorable cards in the tarot.

The Devil card's power derives from restraining sexual energy. When we are aroused but hold back, we feel the Opposer prodding us into action. Our most natural inclination, like the animals, is to be led by our sexuality. But in The Devil card, fire points to the ground, contrary to nature. Strong is the one who can exercise self-control.

Speech

The twenty-two letters and the ten lights find expression in this world through each human being, known in the cosmos as speaker. They are manifested individually through freedom of choice.

WHEEL of FORTUNE.

THE WORLD.

➤ **WHEEL OF FORTUNE, THE WORLD**

The last attribute of the Ten Sefirot—lights is called Malchut, or Kingship, because through the word the king rules. Kingship/Speech is represented by the Wheel of Fortune and The World. These two remaining cards can be seen as the culmination of the twenty-two cards of the Major Arcana because they carry energies from the prior cards, then turn and give birth to the future. These cards represent the physical earth and have a more powerful voice than any other card. People who draw these cards often are being spoken to from heaven.

The World is signified by a naked woman. Its mate, the Wheel of Fortune, is an orb with an armed lion at the top and the Opposer and the snake at the bottom. Upon the disk the four letters TORA are written in the spaces between the four letters of the Name of the Creator, יהוה YHVH. (The same letters TORA also appear in the tarot deck on the scroll in the lap of The High Priestess.)

Both The World and the Wheel of Fortune have a primordial symbol of animal life in each corner: the lion (source of all wild animals); the ox (source of all domesticated animals); the eagle (source of fish and birds); and the human. The culminating voice of all the cards, they have the double meaning of both "earth" and "woman," synonymous with the Goddess energy known as Schina. She is the Godly presence that hovers over us like a bird over her young; she feels our pain and our joy as she quietly accompanies us through the years of our life.

The World card pertains to the speech of the heavens expressed in tangible, physical form in the world. You need not be a venerated person to have heaven speak to you; in fact, heavenly voices come more readily to the simple people; as it is said, "God loves the simple people—that is why there are so many of them." The learned tend to hear the harsh decrees while the rest of the people hear the soft words of the Creator.

The Wheel of Fortune conveys the subtle, intangible speech of heaven. There are certain things that happen in life that have the irrevocable stamp of the Creator. They might be positive in nature or detrimental, but you know whence they came and who sent them.

EACH CARD IN
ITS SUIT

THE FIFTY-SIX CARDS
OF THE MINOR ARCANA

The Minor Arcana in the tarot resembles in structure a deck of playing cards: It has four suits, each consisting of nine number cards from Two through Ten plus a set of royal cards. The Minor Arcana differs from a deck of playing cards in that each of the four suits contains five royal cards: Page, Knight, Queen, King, and Ace.

The anomaly of the missing One is the key to understanding the Minor Arcana. In the tarot, the One is replaced by the five royal cards, representing the five parts of the soul. The number cards Two through Ten represent the nine parts of the body.

Each number card in a suit displays its number through the suit's representative element. For example, the Four of Pentacles displays four coins: Two of the coins are beneath the feet of the prince, one is against his heart, and one is upon his head. Likewise, the Three of Wands depicts three staffs planted by a cliff above a sunlit sea, the rightmost gripped by a man gazing away.

49

In conjunction with their suit correspondences to the four elements, the fifty-six cards of the Minor Arcana can represent or invoke every possible human experience and situation.

The Picture

The tarot cards do not possess particular, restricted meanings. Rather, the tarot cards are the portals to multiple metaphors that can be applied with infinite variation.

Despite the similarities between the Torah and the tarot, there remains an essential difference. God asked the Jewish people to bring the Torah into the world. Not one of its 600,000 characters can be altered or changed in any way. The tarot, while it may be grounded in sacred wisdom, is a human implement, full of imperfections. As with our fellow human beings, when working with the cards it is permitted and even necessary to look beyond their imperfections to discover their underlying truth.

In the sacred text, every letter and gap is a vessel of divine intention and meaning. The tarot cards do not possess that kind of authority. It may be that not every color or number or detail depicted upon the face of each card needs to be interpreted. Not every line and letter in the deck has a relevant meaning. Thus, each card has manifold interpretations, and the cards should be regarded as tentative indications rather than authoritative texts.

THE FOUR SUITS

The four suits of the tarot represent the four elements. Earth is pictured as a coin with a pentacle, or five-pointed star, impressed upon it. Water is depicted as a cup. The two-edged sword symbolizes air. Fire is represented as the wand, or staff.

Of these four symbols assigned to the suits of the tarot deck, only the Coin/Pentacle has value without utility. That is, a staff can be used for walking, a sword for slaying quarry, and a cup for drinking, but the coin is useful only in exchange for something with utility. Thus, the Coin is the most mundane of the suits.

But the coin is valuable because of its metal (its five-pointed star is a sign of Gevurah, hardness and strength), which can be made into a cup or a sword, both implements of consumption. The cup contains the liquid so it can be consumed, the sword cuts through the air and kills the quarry. Water, the Cup, and Air, the Sword, erode earth through the passage of time. By understanding the character of each element, it becomes apparent how the vessel, the element, skews the pure light of the particular Sefira it embodies.

The four elements also relate to direction. Earth is the center, water draws down, air spreads out, and fire goes up. The earth is the nucleus of life; the other three elements hover above. Similarly, the coin, the symbol of earth, provides grounding for our flow, our spirit, and our fire.

The intrinsic value of a person's life is likened to a coin, which can be beaten and molded into a cup. The circle that holds life is described by the rim of the cup and the cone of its sides. Consuming life, or being consumed by life, is how we know life.

The sword, on the other hand, is the line—that which both gives and destroys life. The Sword of the tarot, with two-edged blade, can cut off the superfluous and penetrate the essence.

Whether we consume life inside ourselves using the cup or we consume life outside of ourselves using the sword, we disturb the symmetry of creation as we stride toward the future. Both the Cup and the Sword relate to a future that often slips through the fingers like water or quickly dissipates like air. The Coin, on the other hand, is the undisputed king of the present.

✳ Pentacles—Earth

Life comes from the earth and life eventually returns back to the earth. That time we spend on top of the earth is the span of a life. Each moment of life is the present. The predicament of the human being is being stuck in the present while desiring the future, unlike animals, which dwell in the present and never think of the future. The name for human being in Hebrew is אדם (Adom), a word that can be rearranged to spell מאד (maod), or "more." It is this longing for *more* that distinguishes the human being from the animal, which is satisfied with the present. The steel of the ever-present imprisons the human spirit.

This is symbolized by the Coin, known for its hardness and rigidity.

✳ Cups—Water

The spiritual power of water as expressed through metaphor can be exemplified by the following Talmudic story.

When Rabbi Akiva, one of Israel's greatest sages, was forty years old, he happened to be sitting outside his house after a heavy rain. The water dripped from the roof of his stone house onto a block of limestone. He walked over and examined the stone. It was grooved from the constant wash of the water over many years. "Yes," said Akiva, "I will go and study Torah. Perhaps the Torah will indent me as the water has indented the stone."

Water, the element associated with the suit of Cups, is akin to all the emotions. The nature of emotions, like water, is to be still; what pulls the emotions is the same force that pulls the streams to the sea—unity. The nature of water is that when two drops come together, they become one.

It is the gushing emotion that hollows out our being and makes a place for light to dwell. It is the ephemeral nature of water that works against the hardness. Attitudes and philosophies are broken not so much by logic as by emotion.

The cup restrains liquid's tendency to spread out. The cup has two sides: an inside and an outside. The cup is held by the hand, which itself is a cup. The human being is a cup hollowed out by experience. Some human beings have an elaborate exterior but very little room inside to hold very much. Others may appear coarse yet contain great wisdom.

Once there was a wise man who had very coarse facial features. He was so difficult to look at that a princess asked him, "How is it possible that such beautiful words can come from such an ugly mouth?"

The wise man responded, "In what do you store your wines?"

"In clay."

"Put them into silver."

When the king asked for wine, the servants brought him the wine from the silver containers. The wine had soured. The king demanded an explanation. The servants replied that the princess had commanded them to put the wine into silver containers. The princess said the wise man had told her to do so. The wise man was brought before the king and asked why had he told the princess to put the wine into silver containers.

The wise man explained, "The princess wanted to know how it was possible for beautiful words to come from an ugly vessel. The princess did not know that wine keeps better in clay than in silver."

✳ *Swords—Air*

Between fire and water is air. Air is the invisible, ever-present element. We look at the air and call it heaven. Clouds hang in the heavens and collect water. Like the natural cycle in which water is born out of the clouds and distributed throughout the earth to return back to the sky, the spiritual heavens seed this world with souls and receive them back at death.

The Sword is the tarot symbol for air. The sword of two edges has symbolic meaning in Hebrew: The edge of the sword is called a mouth, because it is with our words that we both express ourselves and protect ourselves.

There is a story about a demon that would come out at night and annoy those studying in the house of learning.

"What shall we do?" asked the students. They decided on a plan. They would invite a wise man to come and speak. When night fell, they would go home, leaving the wise man alone with the demon.

And so they did.

The wise man thought it odd to be invited to teach, only to find himself abandoned at nightfall. He sat down and began to study. Late into the night, he heard a strange sound from behind. He turned and beheld the demon. The thing was short and scaly with six heads. It was putrid green and reeked of swamp gas. The wise man spoke six words in Hebrew that translate as *God, King of saving, save us at the moment that we call*. And the six heads fell off.

In the morning the students returned. They were delighted to be rid of the demon. "We knew you could do it," they told the wise man.

"For this," asked the sage, "you invited me?"

Words rise into the heavens, where angels kiss each word of prayer. A prayer is a thought, emotion, or word directed at the Most High, the Creator of heaven and earth, asking for help. By asking of the Creator instead of bowing down to the elements of reality that appear to sustain us, we make the Creator known in this world.

✳ Wands—Fire

Fire manifests the transfer of earthly light as it returns to the spiritual realm. Erosion is slow fire. The metaphor of fire disappearing into an invisible ether is a physical example of transference between the physical and spiritual realms. Fire melts into the darkness because darkness is the spiritual source of light. Does that make darkness greater than light? The Cabala explains how darkness is greater than light using the example of a ray of sunlight still embedded in the sun prior to being visible.

In heaven, the soul resides in the fiery mass of endless light. Our prayers and praise as we make our way through the complexities of this world feed the fire of the soul. The soul is attached through a thread like an umbilical cord to the body.

The tarot Wand or Staff symbolizes fire. This connects to the highest human aspiration: the future. Whereas an animal stores food for the winter, the human plants seeds. Fire illuminates the future by destroying the present. Fire allows us to explore the darkness. We walk upon the earth and go into the unknown territory. There we make the choices that determine the soul's place in the heavenly chambers.

Once a man took his staff and went out in search of truth. He looked in the cities, searched the institutions, scoured religious and scientific thought, but could not find the truth. He busied himself with business and found time to spend with the indolent, but still he could not find truth.

The man decided to leave the city and go to the country. There he thought he might find someone with a real knowledge who could help him understand the meaning of truth. He found the country dwellers to be independent and spirited. Nonetheless, the knowledge of the country people was ultimately concerned with survival, and had little to do with truth. Truth is the *reason* to survive.

He left the country and went into the wilderness, where he wandered for many years. One day at dusk the man, who had become old and bitter, looked out to the horizon and saw a light. He ran toward the light, feeble and weak. "It must be truth," thought the man.

When he arrived, he found that the light was emanating from a house filled with myriad kinds of lanterns. He entered and saw countless flames attached to wicks floating on oil.

Great silver and gold candelabras illuminated the high vaulted ceiling. Other oil lamps were formed of different metals, more modest vessels were made out of clay. There were decorative lamps and utility lights; there were flames delicately enclosed in glass while others remained open to the wind. The pungent smell of oil was the fragrance of life in each flame that floated on a wick.

A man very much the wanderer's senior appeared before him. "What is this place?" asked the seeker.

"This is the house of the soul," the ancient man answered. "This is where the soul lives."

"Can I see my soul?"

The ancient led him through the labyrinth of lights. The searcher followed, keeping his eyes lifted toward the great lights that illuminated the vaulted ceiling. After all, he had spent his life seeking truth—surely his light must be a lofty one.

The ancient one came to a stop and pointed one long and gnarled finger at a dried-up potato with a crudely carved depression that held the wick and oil. He left the old man alone with his soul. The old man looked at the potato but did not see his flame. The ambient light in the room was too strong and the old man had to cup his hands around the potato to make a shadow.

The old man peered deep into the crevice of the depression in the potato where the oil of his life had been collected. As he looked, he saw a little blue flame about to be extinguished due to the dryness of the wick. Hastily the old man turned to a large vessel filled with oil supporting a brilliant flame that danced like a tongue licking at the heavens, to steal a drop of its oil to feed his pitiful soul.

The shadow of the keeper of the light fell across the back of the old man and a voice called out, "And you are the man searching for truth?"

THE SOUL:
THE ROYAL CARDS

✳ *Ace*

The Ace corresponds to The Hanged Man in the Major Arcana and to *Yachida,* or Oneness—the highest of the five parts of the soul where Pleasure resides. The crown around the head indicates that Pleasure surrounds and can be experienced anywhere in the body. The Hanged Man is hung by the foot, thereby rendering the heart above the head, a sign of Pleasure.

The Ace is the highest of the fourteen cards in each suit, and the hand in Hebrew is associated with the number fourteen. In all four suits, the Ace is shown as a heavenly right hand holding aloft its element (a coin, cup, sword, or wand). As the highest card, the Ace signifies that all things begin with pleasure— our pursuit of pleasure is the source of life.

☞ ACE OF PENTACLES

ACE of PENTACLES.

In the Ace of Pentacles, or Earth, the heavenly hand holds the pentacle above a garden. A hedge divides the garden from the world. At the far side of the garden, a path through a bowered gate leads from the garden to the outside. Beginnings are hard, but they are also beautiful. By leaving one's comfortable surroundings and going out into the world, a person begins the journey into life. These ideas apply to any new venture: to the beginning of love, to new thoughts and attitudes. Children often choose this card.

The Ace of Pentacles is the profound present. The highest part of the soul partakes in the great joy of a new venture. It is why we feel so exhilarated. Because all beginnings are hard, the Creator made the soul infuse the body with the joy of pleasure at the advent of life's changes.

Do not be fooled by the card's pleasant evocations: The sun will set, the wind will howl—things will be difficult. All beginnings are difficult.

➤ ACE OF CUPS

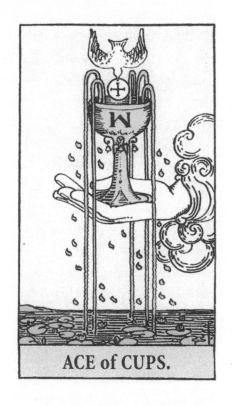

ACE of CUPS.

In the Ace of Cups, or Water, the heavenly hand holds aloft a cup that overflows in four directions. The four directions indicate the earth. Water is a blessing upon the earth. Water moves the earth and changes its contours. A dove descends bearing a coin marked with four directions, which, when dropped into the cup, makes it overflow. Growth comes from water.

A person is inundated by temporal life. At the same time, blessings from the highest level cover the earth. The abundance of water hides what is real and distorts what is seen. Everything is impermanent, flowing, and only change is constant.

Sometimes life just overflows with pleasure from our deepest reservoirs. The seed of our children emanates from that place and sometimes that energy just oozes from us and we are blind to all suffering. Life is unstable, but beautiful. The way we use our pleasure is the name of the game, because the flow of life is predicated upon pleasure.

☛ ACE OF SWORDS

In the Ace of Swords, or Air, a sword raises a crown above the arid land. The growing things that the water nourishes have been cut from the earth and lifted into the heavens. The thumb of the heavenly hand is almost completely hidden in this card, as is the spiritual agenda that imparts the urgency to life.

ACE of SWORDS.

Ultimately, life experience is rendered as a sacrifice to the Almighty. How we grow and what we produce can find justification in their spiritual meaning. The invisible crown of life, the greatest pleasure one can hope to achieve, is the sense of purpose. The purely physical growth quickly returns to the arid earth.

It is the invisible of life, like the space between letters, that separates the oneness of the light into our individual souls. Each person is a particular point in the cosmic labyrinth surrounded by infinite space. It is the space that makes us free. By pondering the invisibility of space, we come to sense the spiritual world that quietly pervades our physical existence. This is the source of life, a pleasure like none other.

☛ ACE OF WANDS

In the Ace of Wands, or Fire, the heavenly hand holds a budding staff (the wood buds with leaves though disconnected from

the ground) above an illuminated landscape. The miraculous budding staff is an
ancient symbol in the Torah
of God's pleasure with us.
Fire is beyond purpose. It
consumes bliss and returns
us to pleasure, the highest of
all aspirations. All the fingers
of the right hand are visible
here.

ACE of WANDS.

This card pertains to
the passions and to thrill-
seeking adventures. Only
the miraculous satisfies the
people drawn to the Ace of
Wands. It is apt to be picked
by people with big plans,
by obsessed artists, and by
people with ideals that far outstretch reality.

I once read for a young man who picked all four Aces. At first I
thought, "This man must be great." Investigation showed me I was
wrong. Stumped as to the meaning of his cards, I asked him what he
did. "Nothing," he said with a blank, drugged-out expression.

"You are not an artist or thinker?" I asked, dumbfounded by the
meaning of the four Aces.

"Nope," he said.

I looked him in the eye and said, "The Ace is a sign of beginning
in all four of the elements. You've got to begin. It does not matter
where you begin because all things are tied together. If you take one
step, the other foot will follow."

✳ King

The King corresponds with the second highest level of the soul, *Chaya,* or gives life. Here resides Will, the male counterpart to Pleasure. In the tarot, each King holds the element that he rules. There is an infinite variety of ways for us to will the elements. Where Pleasure is described as a circle, Will is described as a line. The line points to what is wanted. When the line is hit with spiritual purpose, then direction is established. Knowing what we want is the most difficult part of getting what we need.

➤ KING OF PENTACLES

KING of PENTACLES.

The King of Pentacles, or Earth, is surrounded by darkness, which is accented by the very yellow sky at his back. His throne is decorated with horned heads. It is as if the King, through his will to subjugate the earth and tame the animal beneath his steel foot, has blocked out the light. The desire for physical things can greatly darken one's life because the will required to achieve dominance over things is spiritually the least desirable.

Our will is seen in our power to focus on and see only what we want. When you want one physical thing, it is hard to also pursue another. In the spirit realm this is not so; the more you want, the more you will receive.

✎ KING OF CUPS

The King of Cups, or Water, floats on the waves of the sea, the ship and the serpent behind him. He holds his cup in his right hand and his scepter in his left. Will, the throne on a slab of stone, floats upon water. The ship, in the distance, is a device of man that traverses the sea; the serpent beside his throne is a creature of the water. The King of Cups floats between two options: the security of joining another's journey and dream, and the freedom of being of the sea, letting the

KING of CUPS.

tides bring him to his true destination. This choice, between compromise and freedom, we face many times throughout our lives.

Our will must be malleable before the will of the Creator. Life is often compared to an ocean, in constant turmoil. In order to float and not sink our will must constantly adapt to the will of the Creator. Thank God, we do not always get what we want. Sometimes we don't even get what we need, but it is our will to survive that keeps us afloat while stability draws near. Help comes from both the natural and the fabricated.

✎ KING OF SWORDS

The King of Swords, or Air, sits on a throne that extends above the clouds. Butterflies ornament the backrest of his throne. Two birds fly in the background. This King is both permanently situated and yet completely unencumbered. His will is as clear as his vision.

Will is the fulcrum of freedom; having our will constrained

is as terrifying as having our body restrained. Spiritual Will is quiet but adamant; with spiritual awareness comes the dissolution of doubt.

In the spirit world there is but one Will, the Will of the Creator. When we align ourselves with this Will, we are at peace. Dogma is the counterfeit currency of divine Will.

☛ KING OF WANDS

The King of Wands, or Fire, sits in the desert, his sole companion a lizard in the foreground. The fire animals, lions and salamanders, are carved into his throne. He holds the miraculous budding staff in his hand. His Will burns with passion. Nothing stands before Will.

Air feeds fire. The outcome of spiritual Will is illumination, which is reflected in every part of life. Blind Will can perform miracles, doing the impossible deed, but blind Will can also destroy, so be careful what you believe. Know what is feeding the fire—the pleasure from within and the invisible, the elusive purpose of life, from without.

KING of SWORDS.

KING of WANDS.

✳ Queen

The Queen corresponds with the third level of the soul, *Neshama*, or breathing soul, which informs the intellect. Pleasure and Will comprise the crown upon her head. Inside the head is the brain. The mind constantly produces thoughts because the feet of the essence, the manifested Will, are continually running in the head. The head is where the five parts of the soul attain balance: The two powers of Pleasure and Will and the two external expressions of Emotion and Action merge through the Intellect.

The head is cool and methodical. Intellect translates the messages of the soul into something the body can understand. To accomplish this, the union of fire and water (the fire of the soul in the moist tissue of the brain) produces an electrical impulse to stir the body.

➤ QUEEN OF PENTACLES

The Queen of Pentacles, or Earth, inclines her head toward the Coin, the symbol of Earth, which she holds on her lap. Her throne is situated on a gentle hill in a beautiful garden. Garlands surround her, the sky is illuminated, the distant mountains are blue. This card has affinities for people who, perhaps because of their sensitivities, withdraw to live in intellectual bliss cooled by their thoughts. They are afraid to enter the world, and would rather contemplate it from afar.

QUEEN of PENTACLES.

Some people just live life with their heads in the clouds, a malady I have suffered from throughout my life. With your head in the clouds your body is very vulnerable, but if the body is in a safe place, the head can think enormous thoughts. A pure thought can last a very long time. The Talmud asks, Which is better, thinking or action? The Talmud answers and says that thought is greater because it leads to action.

QUEEN OF CUPS

QUEEN of CUPS.

The Queen of Cups, or Water, raises her vessel, which has become an incense holder. The censer, used during the ritual ending of the Sabbath, is joined to another ancient Jewish symbol: the angel. Two angels face each other from the left and right sides of the covered cup.

The cup, usually an implement of physical consumption, has been transformed into an angelic vessel. The ever-changing seas that lap upon the shore in the card represent life's knowledge. The cup is made to hold a liquid substance. Like a child, we understand the world around us by internalizing it—drinking from the depths of the seas of experience. When the liquid of life is transformed into understanding, we have divested the physical and seen the spiritual skeleton, the bedrock of meaning, that underlies it.

Each of us possesses our own unique knowledge of the world. The Jewish tradition is to argue—we are famous for it—but we argue for the purpose of honing logic, not to proclaim right or wrong. In spiritual things there is no right or wrong; between each being and the Creator there is an independent spiritual reality.

QUEEN OF SWORDS

The Queen of Swords, or Air, rules on a throne decorated with butterflies and a winged head that sits above the clouds. Her robe is sky blue, with clouds and gold piping. Her crown is formed from yellow butterflies. She raises her left palm. The sword that rests on the arm of her throne extends above her head. Her spiritual alacrity rules. She understands the invisible.

The need to attain spiritual knowledge is not the purpose of life, but rather a balance to the physical reality. When we have gone too far, the physical world pushes us into the spiritual. There are times to seek spiritual knowledge to put our lives into perspective.

QUEEN OF WANDS

The Queen of Wands, or Fire, rules upon a throne of lions. In front of her sits a black cat. She holds the budding

QUEEN of SWORDS.

QUEEN of WANDS.

staff in her right hand and a sunflower in her left. She understands both the dark and the light.

Understanding and fire are antithetical, as we can see: The fire of emotion often overcomes the cool logic of the mind. How does one understand what cannot be understood? Here in the Queen of Wands that question finds an answer.

Fire has no beginning and no end, like the spiritual source it seeks. Some people who have a spiritual agenda have an objective: They need to understand. Like a fire, understanding has the most ephemeral boundaries. To understand is to luxuriate in fire. It is a never-ending and constantly spiritual quest.

✳ *Knight*

The Knight corresponds with the second lowest part of the soul, *Ruach,* or "Spirit," manifesting in the emotions. Just as the head balances the spirit world and the physical world, so too the heart is the emotional control center of the body. The emotions wait for permission from the brain to emerge. The emotions animate the limbs. For this reason, the horse is the common symbol of the Knight. In the tarot, each Knight rides a horse—one black, one gray, one white, and one red.

Years ago out West, I drank at a bar with an old cowboy who told me this story:

Once there was a fort under siege by the Natives. The captain asked the scout, a weathered veteran, to ride for help. The nearest fort was three days away. The scout agreed to go, but only if he could take the captain's horse. The scout knew horses. "He ran that

horse for three days straight," said the cowboy. "The moment the scout entered the gate of the fort, the horse keeled over and died. That's how horses are, they'll just run their heart out for you."

It is characteristic of the emotions that they sometimes force us beyond our limits.

➤ KNIGHT OF PENTACLES

The Knight of Pentacles holds the coin in his hand. The sky is yellow, the horse is black. The man is armored but the horse stands still—signifying the emotional darkness within

KNIGHT of PENTACLES.

that makes us sad. Everything around us can be bright, but oftentimes we are immobile. When the emotions don't flow, they hurt; like water, we stagnate.

Trauma impales the emotions. Trauma hides, sometimes for years, then strikes like a snake; its venom immobilizes the prey. Life can be beautiful all around us, but that dark spirit from within can spoil the most ideal scene. It is the past pushing its unwanted self into the present. To overcome the present one must move into the future.

➤ KNIGHT OF CUPS

KNIGHT of CUPS.

The Knight of Cups holds a chalice in his right hand. His colorful attire and shining armor are the emblems of contentment. His horse trots. A stream is before him. He sallies forth into the world. This image conveys the most comfortable of emotions. It exemplifies the standard by which we judge ourselves happy.

Happiness is a state of being; it cannot be measured and quantified. Happiness often has no reason and we cannot give it to others just because we want to.

This is quiescent emotion; yet even at rest the emotions move, because life is not happy standing still. The heart knows there will be time to be still when we die.

KNIGHT OF SWORDS

Astride a white horse, the Knight of Swords gallops against the wind. The clouds are troubled. The man is on a mission, his sword is held high. He personifies the emotion that allows us to stride forward against the adversary.

We often act against our own self-interest, sometimes out of foolishness and sometimes as a sacrifice. It is easy to take what you believe and go into the world and fight for it. It is much harder to fight the belief. There is a constant war in the world we live in between the enlightened and the darkness of ignorance; some fight for what they believe, while others know.

KNIGHT of SWORDS.

Believing is the antithesis of knowing because we may believe in what we do not know. Sometimes belief comes as a result of knowing—we know it is day and we believe that night is right behind; and sometimes belief is a substitute for knowing. Organized religion often falls into that category.

➤KNIGHT OF WANDS

The Knight of Wands on his red horse leaps like fire. This is the portrait of passion. Passion is the state of one's emotions; we can be passionate about anything. The body is the wick of passion's flame. The heart leaps, the breath quickens.

KNIGHT of WANDS.

Our emotions tell us more about ourselves than our thoughts do, because our emotions are often unrestrained and very close to the surface. Thoughts are our hidden world. Unrestrained, fiery emotions are the essence of being alive. But we must be careful in the grip of passion not to hurt anyone.

✳ *Page*

The young man stands on the ground. He is the symbol of the lowest of the five levels of the soul, *Nefesh*, or "creature." Our brain is the fertile soil he treads upon. With all the greatness of Pleasure and Will, with the exactitude of mind and the burst of Emotion, Action is what changes our place upon the earth.

The legs possess little intelligence, but they do have a knack for running and dancing. Because of his insensitivity, the Page, or Soldier, has the toughness to sleep on the ground. His brute courage and stoic determination proceed from a limited understanding. It takes time to accomplish anything worthwhile and it is hard to remove that which we have done or to stop what we put into motion.

☛ PAGE OF PENTACLES

PAGE of PENTACLES.

The Page of Pentacles, or Earth Soldier, holds the coin, and in it he sees all the world. What to do? The land is lush. The trees are tall, and he is a giant. He gazes at the coin and wonders at the infinite opportunities for action.

Unbridled potential is exhilarating, but it is scary. Infinity resides in the vastness of choice—not the common everyday thoughtless choices, but rather those significant moments when the path of our life is set before us by the choice we make in that moment. Sometimes, like the Page, we see the choice in our hand, but the possible outcomes are endless.

PAGE OF CUPS

The Page of Cups, or Water Soldier, stands at the foot of the sea, peering into his chalice. A fish peers back at him. By consuming life, by seeing how life tastes, we come to see who we are. That's what we do with the cup—we taste life. What soldier has not seen life staring back at him from a bottle?

The greatest of all sights is to behold one's purpose as reflected in one's abilities. The person is like a cup: One may be elaborate on the outside but crude within and therefore can hold very little. Nonetheless, every cup holds something. If we look into the cup of our being, the hollow space within, we will perceive our abilities. We will know our purpose because we will see the true reflection of ourselves.

PAGE OF SWORDS

The Page of Swords is the Air Soldier with his sword extended into the clouds. Most

PAGE of CUPS.

PAGE of SWORDS.

action we take is physical and we hope there will be some spiritual effect from our actions. Sometimes it is possible to do something that has no physical, tangible result, but rather profound spiritual reverberations.

The Page is more than just a soldier; he is the royal youth ready to join the earthly battle. The Page of Swords represents the soul at its lower level—coming into the earth to accomplish a spiritual goal. The Cabala teaches that the reason the mind works without pause or cycle is that the feet of the soul constantly run within the brain of the body.

PAGE OF WANDS

The Page of Wands, or Fire Soldier, enters the arid land with his budding staff. The farthest one can walk is into the future. One must be willing to go into the wilderness, the desert, to forsake the lush land and seek the vision.

PAGE of WANDS.

It is said that God created a different work for each person on the earth. Many people work so they can rest, but true satisfaction in life comes not from the rest but from the work. To the Page of Wands, the work is never over.

It is one thing to think the vision and another to impel emotions. But to put the vision into motion is the most profound act, requiring total dedication and commitment. When you see your mission in life, the world becomes like a desert; nothing can quench your thirst but the fulfillment of the action that only you can perform.

THE BODY:
THE NUMBER CARDS

The key to understanding the body of the tarot (the nine numbered cards of the Minor Arcana) is to see them as balancing the soul cards (the royal cards). Balance between soul and body provides perspective; both inform us as to where we are on the path of life, just as the stars guide the sailor.

Each numbered card corresponds to one of the Sefirot. In addition to exploring the relationship between the card and the related Sefira, this chapter will reiterate the Sefira's association with a limb of the body, as well as reveal its color and planet association as inferred from the Zohar.

✳ Two

All the Twos in the Minor Arcana have a connection with The Hermit and The High Priestess, the male and female representations of the left side of the brain in the Major Arcana. Their common link is the attribute of mother, which is called "Builder." The power to build is in increments. Two is rooted in the planet Mercury. Gold is its color. The left lobe of the brain is its limb. This hemisphere is the locus of hearing. The power of understanding is in our ability to listen. Listening and understanding, like building, happen in increments.

The number one is used to refer to the Creator, who pervades Creation but is not part of Creation—the ultimate anomaly. In Creation all things are divisible. The constant state of division characterizes the temporal condition of Creation. The first number that separates the oneness of Creation is two. The cell divides to create a single biological entity, but the unity of that entity separates at death. Oneness is a spiritual quality. What is there in our physical world that cannot be divided?

☙TWO OF PENTACLES

The Two of Pentacles shows a man juggling two coins in a green band shaped like the sign for infinity. At his back are two ships, a large ship going up a wave and a smaller ship going down a wave. The foreground is bare. The Two is pushed by the ebb and flow of life. He stands on the ground and balances his concerns accordingly.

This card corresponds to the left side of the brain, the place of incremental thinking, music, and numbers. Bureaucrats and businessmen excel in left-brain thinking. In matters of love, this card is indecisive. Where decision making is paramount, the rational ability of the left side of the brain both enables and impedes.

☙TWO OF CUPS

On the Two of Cups, a crowned woman and man raise their cups in understanding. They stand under a winged lion's head, which sits atop a staff with a pair of

twined serpents. In the background, a house sits atop a green hill. It is a picture of domestic balance and peace. Mutual understanding is accomplished through recognition of the unique nature of each human being.

There is only one path to equality in this world, and that is respecting and embracing uniqueness. Understanding means to acknowledge without judgment, to admit to the many faces of reality. This is a card of conciliation and mutual respect.

✎TWO OF SWORDS

The Two of Swords shows a woman sitting with her back to the calm sea. Her eyes are blindfolded, she holds two swords in her crossed arms.

This card represents the left side of the brain, called "mother" in Cabala because she gives birth to the emotions. Her attributes are hearing, listening, meditating, and study. She turns her back upon the troubled waters of the world, which seem suddenly calm because she is far away inside herself. She does not see, she does not look. She is hidden like the dark disk of the crescent moon.

Two swords protect her emotions. The nature of the left side of the brain is to go in, close the eyes, and listen. This can be achieved through many forms of meditation, all of them calming. Sometimes the best advice comes from within.

☞TWO OF WANDS

In the Two of Wands, a man stands on the balcony of his home. One staff is fastened to the wall. The other staff he holds aloft. In his right hand he holds the world. The panorama stretches over the green hills to the sea and distant mountains.

True understanding is reflected in the way man esteems his woman and child. The staff in his left hand depicts his wife, whom he holds above himself. In his right hand he holds his child, as expressed in the Torah, "Each person is a small world." Unification of the father, the mother, and the child (what we see, hear, and conclude) completes the intellect.

This is a card of stability, a futuristic desire exemplified by a family in a fortress high above the earth. The earth at their feet is a peaceful, pastoral setting. Stability takes many forms, but the feeling is always the same.

✳ *Three*

In Cabala, One is seen as the dot and Two as the line. The dot of inspiration is elaborated into the line. When three lines meet, they create a triangle, which symbolizes assuredness, or knowing.

All the Threes in the Minor Arcana have a connection with The Hierophant and Justice, the male and female representations of the third eye in the Major Arcana. The three symbolizes "child." It is rooted in the planet Venus. Brass is its color. The cerebellum is its limb.

Knowing connects the head to the heart. Pain is a function of the ability to know: The more we know, the greater our sensitivity to pain.

Knowing accomplishes the cessation of thought. We think to know. When we know, we no longer require thought.

☞ THREE OF PENTACLES

The Three of Pentacles is dark and cavernous. Two authoritarian figures, a man draped in religious robes and a woman in the garb of wizardry, hold a paper between them. This is the doctrine and the dogma of authority. They are telling the aproned apprentice what to know. The boy stands on a bench, to reach their stature. He does not have the knowledge to refute them. He turns his cup down against what they proclaim.

The refutation of dogma is a pointless endeavor because it engages us in the very dogma we wish to divest ourselves of—it is how dogma ensnares us. The good in dogma is what attracts the unsuspecting and beckons them to try to make the dogma better. Do not attempt to turn the lie into the truth, because a crooked thing cannot be made straight. How much of the lie must we see before we abandon it? Fighting doctrinal lies entails as much doctrine as the lie itself.

It is easier to fight over what you believe rather than to know what to fight for. It is easy to get persuaded to a cause and give up individual rights. It is just as easy to give up one's right to fight against the dogma. These are different sides of the same coin. True knowing requires no outside approval; it is personal and without judgment of right or wrong—it is just what we know.

◥THREE OF CUPS

The Three of Cups is a spiral of three strands: three dancing women, each holding a cup above her head. The harvest vines are at their feet. One holds a cluster of grapes. The cups are brought together and elevated. The unity of three, coupled with the element of water, gives rise to a type of knowing that can flow out into the world. The value of the uniqueness of each knowing is represented by the equality of the cups raised together in harmony.

Doubt brings suffering; it is how the emotions become separated from the intellect. Doubt produces unstable emotions void of a course to follow. The Three of Cups conveys the opposite—there is joy because doubt has been overcome and knowing has been achieved.

☛THREE OF SWORDS

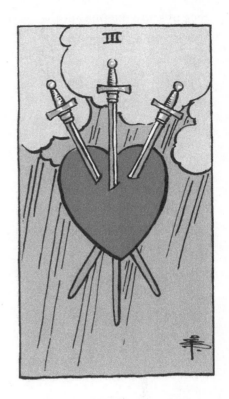

The Three of Swords pierces the heart. Three clouds rain down into the gray. The swords are like those impulses that emerge from the three parts of the brain and enter the heart, initiating emotions. There is a kind of knowledge that cannot be turned aside. Knowing is experience: The more we experience knowing, the more we know.

There is knowing that we share with the world and there is knowing that is internal, personal—a thing that pierces the heart. It is more spirit than substance. It is simple and inexplicable; few people can understand.

☛THREE OF WANDS

The Three of Wands depicts three staffs planted at the end of a long journey. The man looks out and sees three boats sailing on luminous water. In the far distance lies the beginning of another land.

This card is often drawn by people in new relationships or people with far-reaching goals. The process of knowing one another is part of every relationship. How do you know that you know? The answer in the card is this: After a long while, you might see a little bit of the other. It is that little glimpse into another's soul that draws us into the relationship; it is the experience of knowing one another. The act of knowing that we experience in personal relationships we can extrapolate into the world.

Once you know that the thing you have been searching for truly exists, the search becomes much easier. All that divides the two landmasses is the sea, the ocean of life. Once we have seen our objective, reaching it is just a matter of navigating through life's surprises.

✳ *Four*

All Fours in the Minor Arcana have a connection with The Sun and The Star of the Major Arcana. The Sun and The Star are the male and female sides of the attribute Kindness, the first of the six emotions. The Four is rooted in the planet Earth and is expressed through the right arm emanating from the lungs. Its color is blue. Kindness is the beginning of all things. The Creation of the world is considered an act of kindness. Before Creation there was nothing and no external reason to create; it is through the kindness of the Creator that we are continually born into a world of goodness disturbed only by our free choice.

Kindness, the first emotion, is an expansive, life-affirming movement directed outward. This emotion entails the pleasure of giving, and is often confused with love.

Every baby comes into this world with a closed fist as if to say, "This world is mine," and leaves this world with an open hand as if to say, "Take it." While we live, it is good to give with a warm hand. With death the hand opens, but the hand is now cold.

Live to give!

☞ FOUR OF PENTACLES

The Four of Pentacles shows the difficulties that attend giving. A young man sits with coins beneath his feet, a coin held to his chest, and a coin upon his head. He bends from their weight. The city is at his back. He feels compelled to give—in thought, in speech, and in action—but it is hard.

It takes skill to tell the difference between the difficulty of beginning (all beginnings are difficult) and an inappropriate time to begin. The desire to give is often frustrated by the inadequacy of action due to the difficulty of the task.

☛FOUR OF CUPS

In the Four of Cups a young man sits beneath a tree. He stares at three cups that are before him. While he is sitting and thinking, a fourth cup is offered through the hand of providence extended from a cloud.

Sitting is the posture of thought; lying down is the posture of the emotions; standing is the posture of action. The head ruling the heart is a human attribute. Spontaneous occurrences tend to outweigh other considerations. If we give ourselves time to think, the opportunities that appear before us will be joined by the unexpected.

☛FOUR OF SWORDS

In the Four of Swords the man lies upon his back. His hands are poised in prayer. One sword is horizontal beneath him. Three swords hang on the wall, pointing down, next to a stained-glass window.

Beginnings require faith. It is faith that we rely on, and it is with faith that we draw down the light of kindness from the heavens. Compared to faith, thinking is very limited. Faith brings the unexpected. It is good to meditate in our hearts at the beginning of new ventures to discern the possible consequences of our future actions.

✐ FOUR OF WANDS

The Four of Wands depicts the beginning as a couple approaching their marriage canopy, which is supported by four budding staves. The man holds two bouquets but the woman only holds one. Her left hand is barely visible. A fortress stands behind them, and everything is illuminated.

Emotions are hidden within the feminine. Man and woman coming together in marriage celebrates the beginning of a new cycle of life. Every process strives not for the end, but for the new beginning. The only reason to end is so you can begin again: So it is in life and in every aspect of life—oscillating between end and beginning.

✷ *Five*

All Fives in the Minor Arcana have a connection with Death and Judgement of the Major Arcana. They deal with the emotion of holding back and the power of contraction. The essence of strength lies in the heart, a strong contractive muscle that has the ability to stop the flow of blood that is the source for the life force inside the body. The Five is rooted in the planet Mars. Red is its color. The heart, on the left side of the body, is its inner limb while the left arm is its outer expression. Strength, according to the Cabala, is expressed through the left arm.

Whereas the Four depicts beginnings, the Five speaks about endings. The Five ends the cycle. Blood entering the right side of the heart is without vitality. The secret of the heart is rooted in the left. The left contracts and closes. The tired blood builds up pressure and generates heat within the shut chambers of the heart. When the heart stops holding back, the life is over.

☞ FIVE OF PENTACLES

The Five of Pentacles is a bleak scene. Nothing is growing. The only light emanates through the stained-glass window, from within. Outside, a ragged couple passes by. The woman leads, the man follows on crutches, his face to her back. It is winter, the cycle is over. This card is predominantly black and white.

Try to end things with kindness. An ancient tradition in response to death is to tear cloth; both the sound and the action resonate deep within us. When that which has been woven together rips, the spiritual pain is enormous. After the end there will be help; it is shining out into the street. Be assured there is always a future.

FIVE OF CUPS

The Five of Cups features a man dressed in mourning black. Three spilled cups are before him and two standing cups are behind him. There is a bridge across a river, and a house in the distance. Before going on he must deal with what has happened. But not all is lost. When he turns from his mourning, he will face two empty cups and a flowing river.

A new cycle cannot begin unless the old cycle ends. To mourn misdeeds is the best way to remember not to repeat them. Mourning is a way to give respect and acknowledgment to that which we have consumed in ignorance.

FIVE OF SWORDS

The Five of Swords shows the end of a battle. Soldiers have thrown down their swords. They have turned their backs and walk toward the water, defeated. The strong man picks up their swords. He knows as long as the war rages, the battle is never lost. Distress is pictured in the clouds.

War tests one's strength of belief. The smart man gathers the swords after the battle. It takes endurance and fortitude to stand up to adversity. When others give in, be strong because it always produces something. Endure, survive, don't give up.

FIVE OF WANDS

In the Five of Wands, five men hold staffs, each one in a different stance. People meld together through strength and confidence. Confrontation is the test of their convictions.

This is a card of confidence through strength. The most immediate product of "holding your own" is the strength to succeed. All things emerge from darkness; only those who have failed know the true bliss of success.

The Five of Wands is the positive product of difficulty—an inner confidence gained through real experience. We posture ourselves in the world by asserting or adapting. To stand among others we need not be the best or the biggest, just confident about who we are.

✳ *Six*

All Sixes in the Minor Arcana have a connection with The Magician and The Fool of the Major Arcana. Sixes are concerned with compassion, which is related to the attribute of truth that is called Beauty. Like truth, compassion arises from mediation between various opposing factors. It is the combination of kindness and severity that produces compassion; the kind nature holds back for the sake of justice but delivers justice with kindness.

The Six is rooted in the planet Jupiter. Green is its color. The torso is its limb. From the conjunction of the lungs and the heart, the human being connects directly with the Creator. The experience of connection is what we call love. Love, according to the Cabala, is not an emotion, but rather the summation of what we know—either we love it or we fear it.

The torso is the trunk of the limbs where all things merge. The power to merge is embedded in our ability to love, thus represented by the Six. Love emanates from knowing. Knowing pierces into the center of the heart. It is from this point, the center of the heart, that we know the Creator. The heart's ability to love is a reflection of its ability to enter into the oneness of God. In this way, love unites.

☞ SIX OF PENTACLES

In the Six of Pentacles a rich man gives to the poor. He weighs with his left hand and gives with his right to a man who kneels before him. Another kneels and asks, but does not receive. If the rich man really loved the poor, he would not make them kneel.

Relationships are often one-sided. No one should have to beg for love. Real love is unconditional; it is what the child expects from the parent and it is how the parent is tested during the child's teenage years, may God help us! When love becomes intellectual, the heart turns cold.

➤ SIX OF CUPS

In the Six of Cups, the lad bends his knees to the modest maiden because she is smaller than he. He does not wish to tower over her as he offers her a cup of star-shaped flowers. Four more cups filled with flowers stand in the foreground. One cup, behind the young man, is elevated above them.

Love gives deference to the receiver. The great gush of love only gets everyone wet; love needs to seep out, slowly. By containing our love and by offering only what can be received and by showing respect for the receiver, perhaps something can be communicated. Love is the result of restraint that squeezes a drop of pure love from the heart.

➤ SIX OF SWORDS

The Six of Swords shows a man propelling a small boat through the water with a long pole. A woman and a child sit with their backs to the man. Six swords are in the bow of the boat. Water and air merge through the vehicle of the boat.

The man gives deference to the woman and child. He does not require their acknowledgment. Their backs are turned to him—he does what he does out of love.

There are two types of love: a love that has a reason and a love that has no reason. The love that has a reason is a love that will not last because when the reason is gone, so is the love; a love that has no reason is a love that lasts forever.

✒ SIX OF WANDS

The Six of Wands is the ultimate expression of love. A man rides a white horse to the wedding celebration, accompanied by his friends. He holds a staff with a wreath attached to its top. A similar wreath crowns his head. King Solomon wrote in Proverbs "A woman of valor crowns her man." In Song of Songs, he extols the great virtues of woman, comparing the relationship of the Creator and the

Jewish people to a sensitive man making love to a beautiful woman. In order for the woman to crown her man, he must first lift her above himself.

There is no love without respect. Woman is the diminutive of man physically to express the relationship between God and Creation. If man through his physical strength forces himself on a woman, it is rape, but if man holds woman above himself, adapting himself to the needs and pace of the woman, then it is love. The patience of the Creator is without limit—the more selfless the actions of the man, the more he will reap the unbridled love of the woman.

✴ *Seven*

All Sevens in the Minor Arcana have a connection with The Chariot and Strength of the Major Arcana. Seven is the emotion of striding forward into eternity. In the story of Creation, there are six days of Creation and one day of rest; the day of rest is beloved by the Creator and through this love, as the Talmud says, all Sevens are beloved. Seven is imbued with something extra—it is what gives one the strength and fortitude to continually go forward.

The Seven is rooted in the planet Saturn. Violet is its color. The right leg is its limb. From this place the foot strides forward on the earth. The right leg fixes the direction of the body, which confidently puts the strongest foot forward. In the same way that we extend our right hand because it is on the right/kind side of the body, we tend to step out with the right foot—it is how we put our "best foot forward," as the cliché goes.

The attribute of Seven is Victory. Action is many times more difficult than thought and emotion. Even speech is relatively easy compared to action. The spirit of Victory is required to change the world. When we act, we act against what is in place. We must produce momentum to move the status quo, which wants to remain as it is.

☛ SEVEN OF PENTACLES

In the Seven of Pentacles a man tends his vine. He rests his hands upon the implement of work, he rests his head upon his hands: Rest is the antithesis of work. There are many obstacles that turn effort into work. Six of the seven pentacles remain on the tree; only one sits at his feet—it is difficult to get one's money out of one's labor.

The negative side of victory is frustration. In the grip of frustration our goals have become blurry, our resolve shaken, and our energy sapped. It is good to stop and examine what we are putting our effort into.

✏SEVEN OF CUPS

The Seven of Cups depicts the insubstantial hanging in the clouds. The man faces his opportunities. Darkness is at his back. The dragon in the cup on the right could represent the world; the castle represents solitude; the jewels and the wreath are money and power. The cup containing a person's head represents relationships. Danger is a cup with a snake. In the middle is a cup with a secret draped in white surrounded by red. When reflecting upon dreams and aspirations, examine the intention that drives you.

The Seven of Cups mounts seven cups upon the clouds as a symbol of potential. Each cup is filled with a different possibility. It is not substance that is in the cups but dreams. The man faces his potential and has to choose. It is our choices in life and our intention behind the choices that sets our path to the future; sometimes too many choices can be just plain unsettling. Being able to imagine different scenarios and to live them out in the ephemeral world of our waking dreams is one way of finding our way through life.

Once free, we must choose our way in life. Each path has its potential rewards and equivalent dangers. Choosing the insubstantial is far more difficult than making physical choices; choosing our path in life is the hardest. We travel through life like a cup floating on the sea being filled by the rain—do we look to the waves to guide our course or into the sky to plot our future?

SEVEN OF SWORDS

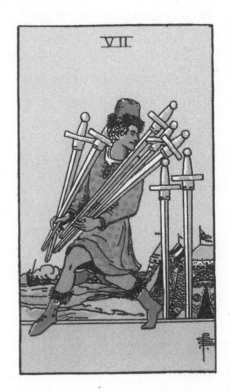

In the Seven of Swords a man carries five swords from an encampment. He leaves two swords stuck in the ground. He steps cautiously away and looks back over his shoulder as if to make sure he slips away undetected. Victory is not always won through confrontation. In every victory there is loss.

In conflict one needs to know when to stop. Victory does not mean annihilation of one's enemy. Victory establishes control, but the ultimate victory is to survive. Live to fight again, that is Victory.

SEVEN OF WANDS

The Seven of Wands shows a man on the high ground. Six staffs oppose his one. Nonetheless, he will be victorious because he occupies the high ground. Victory is not static; true victory is continual. Victory does not mean that the battle is over; victory is just another way of saying that you are not losing.

A good way to deal with adversity is to rise above it. Frustration leads us to set our sights on the future and leave what is adverse. Taking what we can, we ascend to a place where we are no longer vulnerable.

✳ *Eight*

All Eights in the Minor Arcana have a connection with The Moon and Temperance of the Major Arcana. Eight is the emotion of stepping back and the attribute of patience that is called Splendor. In this world everything is competing for attention, which is why male birds are more colorful than female birds. But that which is reticent develops an inner beauty that shines forth through the modest veil of patient waiting.

The Eight is rooted in the planet Uranus, with orange as its color. Its limb is the left leg. The legs are the pillars of our performance, the balancing act we perform upon the earth. When the right leg steps forward, the left leg holds back. This is the hidden strength, Splendor—the woman who inspires courageous acts by men. It is the soft voice of determination within every human spirit, the integral part of the human being that demands integrity and tempers Victory.

People of this nature are quiet, and carry out their deeds without fanfare. They exemplify the inner; they glory in the unseen creative process.

⌁ EIGHT OF PENTACLES

In the Eight of Pentacles a man sits at work, tooling a coin. Another coin is lying by his side and there is one leaning at his foot. Five more coins await his work. The city is far in the distance. The contentment that attends a repetitive job is the opposite of creativity.

A quiet stream can easily be diverted; to be satisfied with the limits of one's nature, no matter how good, breeds subordination. Happiness is not among the higher goals in life; happiness is merely the by-product of a purposeful life. Our work needs to have meaning greater than a paycheck because our work will go on for a lifetime. In every kind of work is the key to all knowledge; to become a master in the spiritual, one must first master a physical form of work.

EIGHT OF CUPS

In the Eight of Cups a man walks along the precipice. The moon eclipses the sun; there is sudden darkness. Eight cups stand stacked in the foreground.

It is difficult to go against conformity and to reject what is familiar. It is dangerous to walk away from order—even familiar oppression, poverty, and dissatisfaction can comfort the fearful of heart. It takes inner strength to leave what is and to walk away into the unknown. Our self-respect is tested by the dangers of the dark as we step away from what is familiar and safe; unwilling to compromise our integrity, we find ourselves on the precipice. These are the times when we learn the most about life if we have the patience for the night and the resolve to stick it out until morning.

EIGHT OF SWORDS

The Eight of Swords pictures a blindfolded woman with hands and legs bound. Eight swords surround her, five on her left and three on her right. She proceeds slowly by testing the waters. She relies on her intuition. Her manner of walking away is to go within. She is protected by the spirit of her actions.

To be nonreactive is the skill of the quiet people who know how to protect themselves by retreating within. They are mothers and children and other sensitive beings quietly moving through a world of confrontation.

☛ EIGHT OF WANDS

The Eight of Wands shows eight staffs pointed down and to the right, suspended against an immense blue sky. A blue stream meanders through a little slice of verdant land. A tiny house sits atop a knoll. Where is the person in this card?

That which stands just beyond our imagination is expressed in a place vacant of ego; the great screen of our imagination is filled with everything but us. As did the Creator of the Universe, in order to create we must first step out of the way and let our action be primary. It is the ego, the I of the person, that needs to sublimate itself to the action.

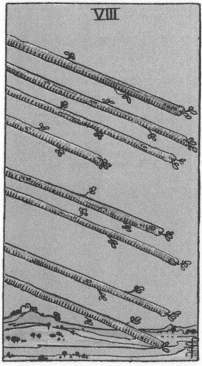

✳ *Nine*

All Nines in the Minor Arcana have a connection with The Lovers and The Devil of the Major Arcana. Nine is Foundation, the emotion that is simultaneously going out and going in. This attribute is connected with sexuality. Sexuality involves the external and the internal, the obvious and the hidden; the sexual act is the most mundane and yet the most extraordinarily intimate. The secret is not a secret if it is revealed, but secret has the allure and possibility of being known. The Nine is rooted in the planet Neptune. Yellow is its color. The genitals are its limb.

Sexual energy is generally directed toward someone or something else. One does not have sex with oneself, even in masturbation one is usually imagining another. The full expression of sexuality requires somebody else. Through sexual energy we discover the profound experience called loneliness.

Sexuality has the unique ability to draw down the most essential information stored in the brain, DNA, and transmit it to a ready receiver along the medium of Will and Pleasure. If there is no one to catch, how will you pitch? In sexuality, we see our incompleteness and our need.

⟣NINE OF PENTACLES

The Nine of Pentacles portrays a young man with his right hand on a stack of six pentacles; to his left are three additional coins. A bird balances on the back of his left hand. Everything around him is verdant and lush. The sky is illuminated. His sexual energy is youthful and always on the brink, ready to fly away.

Sometimes in older people this card can denote casual sex. This card is indicative of fun, but temporal, endeavors. This card is often chosen by children, for they exhibit this energy in its pure form with boundless exuberance. Sexual energy is essentially creative and can take on many forms. Use it well and it will reward you.

✒NINE OF CUPS

In the Nine of Cups the man has become older, his sexuality has matured. Nine cups stand behind him, they are his strength. He folds his hands across his chest and wears a red hat.

The nature of sexuality is to burst out, to overflow the vessel. But virility is seen not in what we put forth, but in what we hold back. The Nine of Cups speaks of the power of restraint.

The virility of man is more apparent when he holds himself back—it is the bow that pulls back the arrow to shoot forth. The more the man holds back, the greater is his virility.

✒NINE OF SWORDS

In the Nine of Swords a man prays before sleeping. Nine horizontal swords hang in the black background.

When we fall we pray, even when we fall asleep. In order to fall, we must let go. Letting go is a sexual energy that comes from deep within—a spiritual sexuality. Fear inhibits this spiritual/sexual energy from being released. Sometimes people are close to what they most want in life but just can't let go of what is familiar and safe. And some people, like a junkie addicted to a narcotic, just can't let go of the junk.

NINE OF WANDS

The Nine of Wands shows a man holding a budding staff while eight other staffs stand erect behind him. He looks wearily over his right shoulder. He requires two hands to hold one staff; more than that is beyond his control. Virility and sexual relationship require constant vigilance to retain their potency.

This card often serves as a barometer in relationship readings. In relationships, the common goal is to be real. Sexuality, more than any other emotion, is real because it is beyond our intellectual control. If there is something wrong in the relationship, the first place it may surface is in the bed. The cabalistic symbol of sexuality is a barrel of honey seeping with fullness, about to explode. Sexual apathy in a relationship is a sign of other troubles that are not being acknowledged and addressed.

✳ *Ten*

All Tens in the Minor Arcana have a connection with the Wheel of Fortune and The World of the Major Arcana. Ten is the spoken emotion, also called Kingship. The king rules with his word—the decree of the king. Words more than anything else distinguish us from the animals, since we have the unique and uncanny ability to articulate thought into words. The Ten is rooted in the planet Pluto. Dark purple is its color. The mouth is its limb.

Man and woman are the conduit to the next generation. The ten is connected to woman more than man. The other nine attributes have male and female aspects, but the tenth represents the uniqueness of woman. Both man and woman give and receive, but only woman gives birth. Speech is symbolic of the birth of the human being by making our thoughts known. Birth is completion; in completion there is rest.

➤ TEN OF PENTACLES

The Ten of Pentacles portrays the Ten Luminaries in their positions on the Tree of Life affixed to the picture of three generations. Animals and plants abound. A young child clings to the skirts of his mother. The woman faces the man, who stands before his father. The structure that surrounds them is complete and secure. But everything is temporal, even completion.

It is time to move on, since the picture for conclusion shows no empty space. After a brief rest, it is time to begin again; one success will surely bring another.

☛ TEN OF CUPS

The Ten of Cups is a celebration. Man and woman stand together and raise their hands to the heavens where ten cups are suspended in a rainbow. Two children dance together. The people and the land are harmonious.

At the end of a cycle it is good to acknowledge what has been achieved. The first step to "going on" is realizing the completion at hand. Take time to acknowledge what you have accomplished and revel in the spiritual meaning of your life—it may not be written in the history books, but it is inscribed forever in the heavens for you and your children.

☛ TEN OF SWORDS

The Ten of Swords is perhaps the most gruesome of all the cards in the tarot deck. A man lays slain by ten swords stuck in a line down the center of his back. Blood flows from his body, the black sky

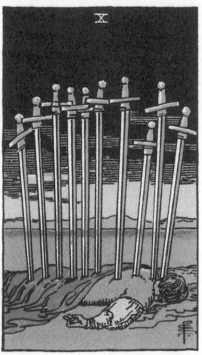

crushes the sunset, the blue of the water and the red of the blood merge.

The head and the spine are the most sensitive parts of the human body. In the Ten of Swords, the slain man symbolizes the male veneer that shields the gentler side of the person from the world. In this picture, male energy, the sword, is turned against itself.

The battle is over, the soldier is dead; and yet the past wants to be heard—wants to touch us at our core and find resolution. In order to be finished with something, we need to allow ourselves to feel it at the innermost level. If we open and allow ourselves to feel, then the past is over and we can proceed more easily to the future.

TEN OF WANDS

The Ten of Wands shows a man walking away carrying ten staffs. The burden bends his back. He is in the service of woman, symbolized by the ten staves he carries. Man holds woman above himself.

With every completion comes the recognition that we serve the purpose of our life. People who think their purpose is within, to satisfy their own needs, end up serving themselves—which is a fruitless endeavor.

If we are good at what we do, we must do more—our ability obligates us to serve. The purpose of our life is our master. The accolades that come with mastery are unimportant.

THE CABALISTIC READING

THE CARDS REVEAL THEIR SECRETS

Learning to read the tarot cards from a cabalistic perspective has been a journey of discovery for me. It began when I returned to my apartment on the day I bought my first tarot deck. I anxiously tore open the box and spread the cards out before me, one by one. I saw seventy-eight picture cards and a small booklet. I threw away the booklet because the cards do not have definitive meanings. When I finished laying out the cards, one thing was obvious: The cards *were* cabalistic in nature.

First, I saw that each of the four suits represented the merging of the ten parts of the body with the five parts of the soul. Then I recognized the correspondence of the twenty-two cards of the Major Arcana to the twenty-two letters of the Hebrew alphabet. But in what way should the cards be read?

I separated the Minor Arcana suits into individual packs according to my Virgoan nature. I saw no reason to divide the Major Arcana cards, so I was left with five stacks of cards. I decided to draw one card from each stack. As a result of my Torah studies, I understood that chance is a thing beyond logic, as is the soul. Since Cabala is the language of the soul, I reasoned, perhaps the cards could convey a message from my soul.

I shuffled through the deck of Pentacles and drew out the Five. It shows a woman walking away from an injured man because life was just too hard with him. It is night. The frozen snow lights their world. The only color comes from what they believe, as pictured in the stained-glass window. Beyond the image—which seemed like a perfect pick, considering my recent divorce—I went further into the interpretation of this card.

The Five is related to the strong side of the heart, whose contractive powers stop the flow of blood thus ending the cycle and allowing a new beginning. Everything in life cycles, nothing remains the same. I sat and stared at this card and thought of the breakup of my marriage and my home. Beyond the simple meaning of the picture, my sense that this card derives from the upper left emotion called Gevurah—Strength helped me interpret its meaning. It takes strength to be poor and alone and survive.

Next I chose from the stack of Cups and randomly selected the Six. The scene depicted two children interacting; the boy was bending his knees to the girl so as not to tower over her while she accepts his cup of flowers. I thought of my own children and how their delicate lives were being torn apart by the divorce. Yes, I thought, if I focus on the needs of my children, I won't feel so much the bleakness of my own situation.

Then I chose from the Swords: the Knight galloping against the wind—my emotional soul. Unquestionably, my battle was with the invisible enemy, the power that persuades good human beings into evil deeds. That was the reason I left Israel to come back to America—I was going to change the world from its fulcrum.

I sat and stared at the three cards that I had drawn. I placed the Five of Pentacles right in front of me because earth, the Pentacle, is the undeniable present. I placed the Six of Cups above it and to the right because water displays the attribute of Kindness like a river carries the present downstream into the future. It is when we find ourselves in the flow of life that Kindness prevails, and Kindness is situated on the upper right side in the Tree of Life.

The Knight of Swords I put above and to the left of the Pentacle, the position of Severity in the Tree of Life, because air displays the attribute of contracting and becoming invisible.

I had yet to draw a card from the Wands, and one card from the Major Arcana, and I could see the Tree of Life pattern forming as three pillars: left, right, and center began to emerge. I decided to first place the remaining stacks along the center pillar and then draw my cards.

Both the wind and the water are ways by which the earth erodes and transforms into something else. The future arises from the ruins. The element of the future is fire, represented by the Wands. I placed the stack of Wands in the center above the other three piles, making a diamond shape out of the four elements: earth, water, air, and fire. Finally, in a stack above the other four, I placed the Major Arcana. The configuration made sense to me, Earth/Present being closest to me; Water and Air would be above and equal; Fire was the culmination, in the center and aloft. Above them all was the soul.

It was time to choose another card. I drew from the stack of Wands and picked the Four. A man and woman are going to the marriage canopy, the cycle is beginning anew.

As I looked at the diamond shape made by the four suit cards, I understood the meaning of the message they conveyed.

In the bleak picture of the Five of Pentacles I recognized my present bitter situation. The Six of Cups and the Knight of Swords spoke of the means to rectify my situation: service to my children while championing the ideal. These two elements were the sides of the ladder that would raise me from the pit. The Four of Wands was the future; the future held a new beginning.

The future never seems to arrive—it is always supplanted by the present. But one day the future does come if we continue along the path. Seeing my path, though it was to be a long and difficult one, gave me solace. I wondered what surprise the Major Arcana held, and how it would modify the whole picture presented by the four suits.

I chose The Sun card, the card of Kindness. It radiated down upon the four suits like the soul radiates down upon the body. At that moment, I realized the meaning of the Major Arcana: It conveys the soul's influence on the body. This was my soul's way of picturing itself. Reacting to the difficulty of my situation, my soul was pouring kindness down upon me.

The darker the despair, the more profound the light. I knew then that the tarot works.

BECOMING A READER
WITH INTENTION

Right around the time that I discovered the tarot, I lost my pants. My children, while on a visit, had done the laundry and returned home without my clothes.

First I had lost my wife, then I had lost my job, and now I had lost my pants. I only mention my pants because in the ten years since they disappeared I have never found another job or another wife, and the pants I wear are a ten-year-old patchwork quilt of anarchic design. I was a man with nothing: What a fool.

But there is value in having nothing. The concept of nothing is key to the tarot, and to the Cabala. In nothingness we acknowledge God. Nothingness is best exemplified in the card known as The Fool. In the twenty-two cards of the Major Arcana, The Fool counts as zero. It represents the innermost emotion of Beauty/ Truth/ Compassion and the closest connection with the Creator. The difference between zero and one is greater than the distance between one and infinity.

I was The Fool striding over the cliff, a flower in my hand. Yes, I knew that card well. God was always challenging me to step into the uncertainty of nothingness. Once again I took the plunge—and embarked upon my career as a tarot card reader.

The knowledge of the tarot is the knowledge of the Torah. Three thousand years ago God asked the Jewish people to bring the Torah into the world and teach it to the masses. I took my last fifty bucks, went to the mall and bought two pairs of Levis, then headed into Manhattan to seek my future. I envisioned bringing something deeply spiritual, the tarot cards, into a pit of modern-day depravity as a sort of art form. So I began reading cards at the Limelight, a seedy club in lower Manhattan notorious for scandalous parties.

Located inside a converted church in lower Manhattan just down the street from the Chelsea Hotel, which Andy Warhol made famous, the Limelight was a high-ceilinged cavern of chambers with belfries and corridors that all led to dark and unspeakable places. It seemed an appropriate place to try out my skill.

There's an old adage quoted in the Talmud, "Much have I learned from my teachers, but most have I learned from my students." Reading tarot and particularly my time in the clubs taught me to respect human beings in all their diverse manifestations. Every human being had a story, had hopes and aspirations. Every soul has purpose in the body; every struggle is holy. There is no path void of God.

The trick to reading the tarot is to always remain empty of preconceived notions. The reader is the intermediary, the conduit or medium through which the message is delivered. The reader should always be The Fool about to step over the cliff. The reader needs to stand in the emptiness of space and wait to be directed by the cards.

When I begin a reading, I straighten my back and become silent. My intention is to be a good messenger of the soul's knowledge to the body.

Intention, the focusing of energy, is the product of meticulously administered will. To intend good is the fulcrum of every reading. Intention keeps the reader in that nothing space. The tarot cards do not predict the future or divine some outcome. The cards tell a story, show a journey, mirror the metaphor appropriate to the subject's unique combination of body and soul.

In the smoky caverns of the New York nightclubs, I got into the habit of counting the cards when I took them out and when I put them away. It is said that God counts each star, taking them out of the sky in the morning and putting them back in the evening. Why does God count the stars? God created the stars. God counts the stars because God loves them. Likewise, it is an act of love and respect to count and look upon each card before reading.

The tarot's story and message are drawn from the deck by the person whose cards are being read. The connection between the soul and the cards depends upon the subject's random choices. After a reading, if someone remarks to me, "Why, that's exactly what's going on," I reply, "You chose the cards. I only read them."

The most bizarre reading I ever did took place at the yearly gathering in commemoration of the original Woodstock Festival. Wandering about the crowd of celebrants, I was invited to a small converted painted school bus. The interior was finished with polished wood and fitted with a small wood-burning stove.

Five or six of us were just hanging around having a good time, feeling like we had been friends forever, when I mentioned that I read tarot.

"Can you read my bus?" asked my host, who was sitting at the driver's seat.

"Everything has a soul," I answered.

I laid out the cards and announced that I would choose the cards for the bus, since it was incapable of choosing for itself. The card at the top was The Chariot card from the Major Arcana, signifying victory. The rest of the cards showed an inward reluctance to move forward.

"Victory is in the right leg," I said. "It is the right leg that presses the accelerator and applies the brake. Yet the vehicle is reluctant."

The driver turned to face me, swinging his legs out from under the dashboard. I saw he had a cast on his right foot.

"It's obvious," I said, "your bus realizes your infirmity and wants you to go slow."

A LAYOUT EVOLVES

Typically I begin a reading with an explanation of the five components: earth, water, air, fire, and spirit. I then go on to point out that all things that begin as earth become eroded by water and air and finally disappear through fire. Above the four elements is the spiritual energy. This was the layout I had devised on my first foray into reading the cards.

But in the nightclubs, I came to the realization that I needed to read ten cards instead of five. After all, the cabalists divide the human body into ten domains as pictured on the Tree of Life. Ten would be a true mirror image of the human predicament. So I added five cards to the layout I had devised. Four of these cards I drew from the Swords and the Cups, two of each, to give the reading more information about the process of the present becoming the future. The last and final card I drew from The Wands to show what can be derived from this process.

To conduct a reading, I lay the four suits and the Major Arcana in individual piles, five in all, and stack them in front of me. I ask the subject to choose five cards, one from each of the five decks. After he or she chooses each card, I direct the subject to place the card on top of the pile from which it was drawn without changing the direction of the card. This erects the skeleton of the reading: one card from each suit and one from the Major Arcana. After each reading, I return the cards to the deck, which I cut once or twice but never shuffle.

There is no proper place in the layout to begin a reading, since all aspects of the reading are equally tied together. It is the reader's responsibility to convey the structure, story, and message of the cards. Sometimes I begin a reading by talking about the soul. I explain how we are made of four physical elements and one spiri-

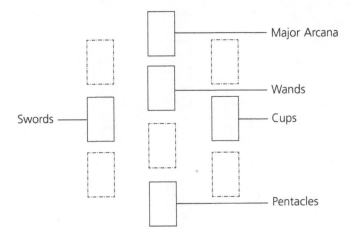

Preliminary layout

tual element. I then explain the Major Arcana card the subject has chosen in terms of the soul. The direction, either feet first (upright) or head first (upside-down), that the soul card (the Pentacle card) descends to earth should be noted, as it speaks to the subject's present state in the world. From stories in the Torah it is known that the soul enters the body head first in the same way the body of the baby enters the world head first; a feet first birth is hard and difficult. The Major Arcana coming feet first indicates a very strong soul influence that can be disquieting.

Sometimes, I show the future next, the fire card. Life is about taking the darkness of the present and transforming it into the fire of the future. I can then show the process of transmuting life through the water and air cards. When the person whose cards are being read can see the explanation in the first five cards he or she chose, it is time to continue the reading.

After we have read the first five cards, I have the subject draw four more cards, two from the Cups and two from the Swords. One card from each pair is placed above the pile for its suit and the other card below the pile. These six cards pertaining to water and air show the way and the means to achieving the future. Again, the

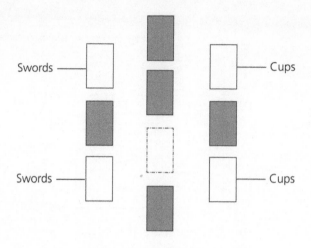

Addition of water and air cards

direction of the cards chosen indicates the nuances of the tarot story. The elements of a reading fit together in countless ways because the myriad combinations of cards can point in so many different directions. The individual's transformation of present into future is depicted in these six cards.

The future is what we strive for, but the reward of the future is the outcome. The last card is drawn from fire, the Wands. This card I place in the space between the cards previously chosen from the fire (Wands) and earth (Pentacle). This card points to the outcome from the future—the benefit we reap from reaching our goals.

The layout now rises up on both sides of the Pentacle, three Cups on the right side and three Swords on the left side, resembling the Tree of Life. The jewel at the top of the crown is the card drawn from the Major Arcana.

A few years after I had begun reading cards, I discovered that if I angled the top and bottom cards from the column of air and the column of water forty-five degrees, a new form arose: a circle pierced by a line, the most profound of cabalistic primal images. Because the tarot cards are a spiritual language, whatever nuance can be incorporated into the physical layout aids in clarity. To see

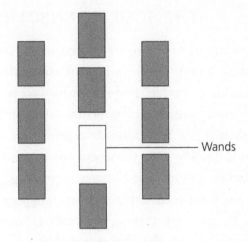

Addition of the fire card

the symbol of man and woman—the line and the circle—balanced and intertwined within the cards perfects the configuration.

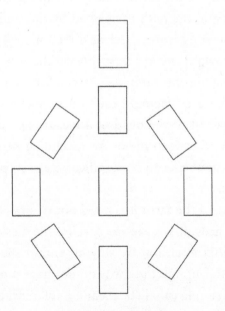

*Angling the cards to form
a circle pierced by a line*

THE SOUL CONNECTION

It is an enormous honor to be invited inside someone else's being, to share with him or her the intense meaning of life. Like the snow-flake, each life is unique. Fulfillment for one is slavery for another. The tarot card reading exacts no moral judgment and pushes no creed; rather, it is a brief glimpse at the human design: a vessel of life spinning quickly upon the wheel of fortune a moment before the potter touches the clay and changes everything.

Since the tarot cards are a spiritual language, a language under-standable by the soul, turning the cards randomly allows the soul to communicate with the body through the medium of the reader. If the reader has a coherent way of understanding the ten divisions of life as expressed in the four physical elements of reality, then the message of the soul will become coherent. Coherence, more than anything else, soothes the anxious spirit.

There is no greater human need than our need for meaning. It is the responsibility of the tarot reader to help the subject see coher-ence and meaning in the path prescribed by the soul.

Often the reading assumes a clear direction, arising out of earth and going first toward the air, then toward the water, or vice versa. Cards that are facing the same direction—for example, feet at the top—or cards that are "facing" each other, such as the head of an upright card adjacent to the head of a feet first card above it, indi-cate a relationship between them. An ascending or descending pat-tern in the card numbers can be significant, as can patterns of color among the cards.

In the reading of the tarot it is good not to stray from the simple meaning of the cards. It is easier to develop the message and remain true to the original intention by staying within the simple param-eters of each card. Though the cards do not have a precise meaning, they do have the simple cabalistic meaning referenced by the picture. The subtle nuances derived during the reading should not contradict the simple meaning of the picture.

An important factor in reading the cards is the meaning of "reversed" cards—those that are drawn upside down. Pay close attention to the direction in which the soul's energy descends through the cards. Some cards are very strong and come feet first. A strong burst of spiritual energy can be very disconcerting when suddenly manifested. By pointing this out to the subject, the reader can give the comfort of reason concerning unsettling feelings that arise without evident cause.

As I have stated earlier, spirituality prefers to come into this world head first, as babies are supposed to come. When water descends to the earth, it does so by condensing into raindrops. This is how water comes upside down. If it did not, we would be flooded. Likewise, the numbered cards of the Minor Arcana, which pertain to the body, act in the way of substance and descend feet first. If they come head first, they signify too much is happening too quickly, and the result can be unpleasant.

Be wary of the temptation to intervene in the events that may be shadowed by the cards. Interpretation of the cards does not presume any action is warranted. Take a subtle lesson from the following story.

Once there was a sage who lived in a cabin deep in the woods. Because the sage was renowned for his wisdom, people sought him out for advice. In order to manage the crowds at his doorstep, the wise man was forced to employ a young man to greet and escort the visitors to and fro.

It happened once that a rich man sought the wise man's counsel. After the visitor's departure, the young man entered and found the sage sitting in silent turmoil.

"What is the problem?" asked the young man.

"He is going out to his death," replied the elder.

The young man immediately ran into the dark forest after the rich man. The rich man recognized the wise man's aide, and was easily persuaded to return to the cabin. On the way

back they passed a soldier cleaning his gun, which acciden-
tally fired and shot the rich man through the heart.

The young man ran back to his master and prostrated himself before him, begging, "Please forgive me. If not for me, the
man would yet live."

"No," the wise man assured him. "The man's time was up,
but you interfered with the good that would have come from
his death. The rich man was to be killed by the local robbers.
Since he is a rich man, the authorities would have gotten
involved and the robbers would have been captured. Now,
because of you, no good comes from his death."

Often the cards show a predilection toward the spirit with a major-
ity of reversed cards. But what is good for the soul is not always
good for the body. Spiritual wisdom is often attained at the expense
of mundane enjoyment and physical comfort. Yet achieving a spiritual goal sometimes leads to fixing a physical problem—it is through
the holes in the soul that sickness enters the body. The opposite is
also true, that by fixing the earth, one can repair the soul.

The up-or-down orientation of the last card chosen and placed
in the middle of the circle can sometimes indicate the dominant configuration of one's life: the circle or the line. The reader's articulation
of the soul's advice to the subject can either be "Return to fix the
past" (the circle, indicated by a card facing up) or "Go away into
the future"(the line, for an upside-down card). It takes tact and
sensitivity to a subject's individual presence to read the soul's advice
to the body through the tarot deck.

I've learned to wait for the whole picture to emerge before
offering my final opinion on a person's cards. Certain aspects of
the cards are altered when nearby cards are turned up in an opposing direction. For example, the Pentacle can often suggest that the
present is undesirable. Reversed, the Pentacle can indicate emerging from the past. Cards that are walking away from one thing are
necessarily walking toward another. Nearby cards can offer clues

to the reader as to what the subject will be walking toward.

Relationships among the cards emerge throughout the reading. Some cards are similar in color; others have a common number and thus share an attribute. These factors do not fully disclose themselves until all the cards have been turned. Reading the cards requires the skill to see patterns and subtle shifts that turn the story and reveal the metaphor of the message.

The Tarot Illuminates Life

The Wise Man

The same sage who foresaw the death of the rich man by the hand of bandits one day locked himself in his room and cried aloud. The crying and pleading went on for many hours until finally, late into the night, pale and drawn, the wise man emerged from his room. He asked his young assistant to find the last person who had visited him.

The wise man's attendant had turned away so many people from his master's door during this demonstration of grief that he could not recall the last person admitted to the sage's presence.

Years passed. The young man grew old in service to the wise man. One day, he took the liberty of asking his master what had elicited such a demonstration of grief so many years ago. The ancient one looked up, his ragged voice almost a whisper from years of dispensing advice. He smiled.

"Yes," said the sage. "I remember. That man I wailed for came to me having committed a very grave offense. He had had sex with a dead woman."

The servant was stunned. Why had his master cried so bitterly over another man's offense? Unbidden, the wise man explained: "In order to give advice, a person must be able to find the same offense within himself. This man came to me with such a gruesome offense, and surely that same offense had to dwell somewhere inside me."

For a long time the servant and the master sat in a twilit silence. Unable to restrain himself before total darkness descended, the servant asked, "So what did you find in yourself?"

The wise man looked compassionately upon his servant and answered, "I talk when people don't listen."

Every reading teaches me about the cards through the human stories they reflect. Every time I put down my table so I can sit and receive people, I learn about our society. I have learned about who owns the sidewalks and who governs the parks. I have learned about ordinances and laws. I've discovered that the police are always happy to teach a person a little bit more.

Most of the tarot cards depict exterior scenes: settings beneath a tree, by a river, under the streaming clouds. On the road, the moon and the sun are the variable constants attending the journey. Both the road and the tarot cards are theaters of the random, the unforeseen, the serendipitous. On the road, I have come to understand the great enjoyment the Creator has in the individual, how the individual journey through life is always fraught with difficulty. Sometimes we oppose God and sometimes God is the opposer. To the reader as well as to the subject, life takes on a different meaning as a result of the tarot cards. The future becomes more evident, the definitive present less tyrannical. The cards make it possible to lead a life based upon spiritual knowledge.

A tarot reading affirms the importance of every individual life, because it is an overt expression of the symbiotic relationship between the soul and the body. The basic difference between the body and the soul resides in mobility: The soul stands while the body walks. The secret of life and death is embodied in the metaphor of the candle and its flame. The body is the candle, the soul the flame. The flame may move, but it is the candle that governs the movement of the flame.

It is by consuming the elements of the candle that the flame moves. That which is consumed, dies—life is consumed to feed the flame of the soul. The future of all things is to become light. Only when connected to a body can the soul move and draw closer to the Creator, because only in the physical world is there found freedom of choice. For this reason, the soul communicates only beneficial messages to the body.

From a cabalist's perspective, the head communes with two places at once. It is connected to the earth through the body; that same body also elevates the head into the heavens.

Thinking is a heavenly process. Thoughts, like spirit, cannot be weighed or detected. The mind can go as far and as deep into the spirit world as the Will dictates. This hidden spirit world is then revealed through speech.

Through speech we change the world. Although we think that we understand, we do not *know* until we speak.

The following records a tarot card reading I did for myself. Instead of talking out loud to the subject, I wrote down what I would say to myself if I were sitting across from me.

Woodstock, N.Y.: 4:20 P.M.

Every reading takes place in an environment called: Where are you? The answer to this question has many sides: Where are you in the world? Where are you in your life? Where are you in your dreams and aspirations? Where are you in time?

Today, as I write, I am sitting in a twenty-two-foot trailer in Woodstock, New York. I have been living here for one day short of the fourteen-month anniversary since I burned down my house through a careless mistake and was forced to take refuge in the middle of the winter. Fourteen is the numerical value of the Hebrew word Dovid. I am fifty-six years old. I am about to complete a book that I have been working on throughout the winter. It is 4:20 in the afternoon.

I open the antique cigar box where I keep my first deck of cards. The pictures are worn. I retired these cards many years ago. The deck is like an old friend, a beloved book filled with memories of intense relationships with countless people, each with a beautiful soul.

I pick up the cards and begin to count them out.

My intention is to be a good reader; there are no bad readings, only bad readers. I close my eyes and in my mind call to God, who knows all thoughts and hearts, to help me.

I count out fourteen cards of Wands, cut them twice to preserve their randomness, and place them in the center.

Next I count the twenty-two cards of the Major Arcana and place them vertically above the stack of Wands.

I place the fourteen cards of the Pentacles at the bottom of the vertical line made by the three piles: the Pentacles, a space, Wands, and Major Arcana.

In the space and to the right I place the fourteen Cup cards. The Swords I place in the space but to the left, opposite the Cups.

I prefer to choose first from the Major Arcana.

I take the deck into my hands and riffle through the cards until one calls out to me and I take it and turn it over. It is The Devil upside down.

The energy of The Devil card derives from sexuality being restrained, as depicted by the horned monster holding the naked man and woman in chains. The root of all creative energy is sexuality. I have been girding my loins for years. As this card is upside down, I can interpret its energy as spiritually instructive.

My soul is energizing me with the power I need to accomplish my task, the writing of this book. Sustained creative energy comes from deep reservoirs. It is this The Devil card protects.

Next I take the stack of Pentacles into my hands. The Pentacles, depicting earth, represent present reality—the place I occupy on the earth.

A card calls out, but its voice quickly fades before I can choose it. I take another card instead and turn it over: It is The Knight of Pentacles.

The sky is illuminated and the ground is fertile, but The Knight of Pentacles is dark and unmoving. His horse is black, so is his armor. He stares at the Pentacle he holds in his hands. He is ready to battle, but has nowhere to go. My soul's creative/sexual energies are restrained; my emotional spirit is unmoving, awaiting the culmination of my task; my own endeavor awaits fulfillment.

Troubling emotions arise in stillness. Emotions must move or they hurt. Just as sexual energy can elicit untrue emotions feigning love, so too the holding back of spiritual/ sexual/creative energy can immobilize the heart at its very source. Finishing a writing project has always left me dispirited. Depression ensues because purpose and direction are yet unrequited.

Next I choose from the Wands.

Since I have uncovered the soul's energy and my present predicament and personal dilemmas through The Devil and Knight, I would like to see where I am going. I take the stack of Wands into my hands. I cut the cards and take the top card.

It is the Seven, the card of Victory.

A man stands on the high ground. With his one staff he protects himself from six enemies. I grew up in the hills of San Francisco, where we would amuse ourselves with rock fights. It did not take long to realize that the higher the ground, the easier the battle.

There is a special wisdom in the action of this card, particularly since it is a card of Victory. Victory is generally thought of as celebration and peace, but the Seven of Wands is actively battling his foes. Where is the victory?

All three cards depict battle: The Devil is the battle against one's nature, The Knight faces dispirited emotions at the end of the battle, the Seven shows the reward of victory—the high ground. Victory is a state of being, not a point in time. Victory means you stand up and protect what is yours; victory moves forward without fear.

For years I have been at war with the world. Perhaps that is why the soul is holding back her strongest energy, to weaken the spirit of the heart and to force the person to take account of his own self. It is one thing to do battle with the world and quite another to let the world do battle with you.

The colors of these three cards—The Devil, The Knight of Pentacles, and the Seven of Wands—read in the order they were turned, suggest a great deal. The Devil (soul) is flesh and black; The Knight (present) is black surrounded by light; the Seven of Wands (future) features more moderate colors, blue and green. Darkness is being eradicated. The man has gotten down off his horse, has taken off his armor, and is facing what opposes him. The bridge from the present to the future is through process.

Since The Knight of Pentacles is a spirit card and not one of the nine body cards, it leads me to choose from the Swords, because they are of the air, the world of thought just below the spirit world.

I turn up the Three of Swords, representing the third eye, knowledge of the spiritual. It is that knowledge with which I write this book. But finishing a book is very different from writing a book; where writing is a fluid, meandering process, finishing a book is the crown of perfection.

Three blue swords from the right, left, and center pierce the red heart. The advice seems obvious. I must allow the spiritual knowledge that I have accumulated in my head to enter my heart. That would help me to get down off my horse and overcome the dark spirit of unfulfilled dreams.

Next, I choose a card from the fifth stack, the Cups. The Nine of Cups, reversed, completes the five-card spread, one of each element and the Major Arcana.

The Nine of Cups refers to sexuality as represented by a seated, middle-aged man. Nine cups are lined up behind him. His hands are crossed upon his chest. Here is the picture of virility: "Strong is the man who can hold himself back." Being reversed, the Nine of Cups reflects more of a spiritual than physical virility—a type of mental alacrity.

Both the Nine of Cups (sexuality) and the Three of Swords (knowing, the third eye) are found in the center of the body. I need to stay centered and true, a message that could apply for a long time and in many different circumstances.

Looking at these five cards as a composite, the reading appears to emerge from the Pentacle to the Sword. A turn in the Cups (the reversed Nine) leads to the Wands and Victory. This is what my soul wishes to accomplish. By holding back, essential energy will be translated into virility, as the present is transformed into the future.

There is a correlation between the Nine of Cups and The Devil: Both sit and both restrain sexual energy. This quality brings the man to the high ground and victory. I also see a progression from the indecision of The Knight on horseback through the patience practiced to retain virility directed by spiritual wisdom centered in the third eye.

To better understand how to connect my spiritual knowledge to my heart, I take two cards from the stack of Swords. Leaving the already turned top card in its place, I take the pack and choose two cards. I place the Ten of Swords at an angle with the right bottom point of the card touching The Knight and the upper right corner of the card touching the Three of Swords. The Two of Swords is placed above the Three of Swords at a mirroring angle. It touches both the Seven of Wands and the Three of Swords.

When we die, the delicate thread of life that connects the body to the soul is cut and the consciousness of the person at the end of the tether of light begins its journey back to the soul. Completing a long task like writing a book is both joyful and terrifying. The completion pictured in the Ten of Swords is similar to what doctors call "postpartum depression," which occurs for the mother after birth. Acknowledging that this is the end of the book allows the Three of Swords, portraying the third eye, which connects the mind to the emotions, to meld into a conclusion. How does an artist know when the work is over? He just knows.

The Two of Swords translates knowing into understanding. The woman is blindfolded—a sign of hearing and intuition, an understanding deeper than what can be seen. She turns her back on the world (the water) and translates what she knows into words.

The predominance of black connects The Devil, The Knight of Pentacles, and the Ten of Swords. The holding back of light and essential energy in the soul and the indecisive nature of the present are shortly to come to an end. The book is about to become completed. Through this process I will come to a turn in my life that will strengthen me and ultimately lead me to victory.

To find out how, I turn over two cards from the stack of Cups and place them one above and one below. In the upper right-hand side of the reading, The Page of Cups tilts upward and left toward the Seven of Wands, while the Seven of Cups at the bottom tilts down and left to touch The Knight of Pentacles.

The symmetry of the reading is broken by the Seven of Cups being turned toward The Knight of Pentacles. There I find an answer to the indecision of The Knight: Reflect upon your dreams and aspirations. Completing brings about new ideas and fresh dreams. Like the Seven of Wands, the Seven of Cups depicts Victory—the victory of following our dreams, exploring endless possibilities.

The Page of Cups stands before the sea and looks into his cup. A fish looks back at him. Between Sexuality (the Nine of Cups) and Victory (the Seven of Wands) lives the fifth and lowest part of the soul, which stands in the head of the person and initiates action. A person is like a cup that is replenished: As one project comes to an end, another stares back at me; the finishing of one book ultimately leads to the beginning of another.

The tenth and last card, drawn from the stack of Wands, speaks of the result that will unfold in the future. It addresses the purpose of achieving the high ground of Victory.

Leaving the top card in its place, I take the pile into my hands and choose one card. I go through the deck, one by one, until a card attracts me. I turn it over and place it in the middle of the circle described by the eight cards of the four suits.

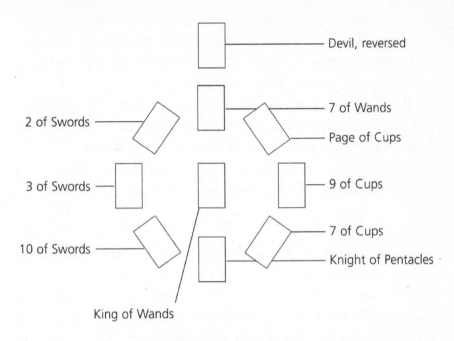

My March 2001 reading

It is the King of Wands, reversed.

The reversal of the spiritual cards, those five cards referring to the five parts of the soul, is a productive sign. The last card drawn, if reversed, also gives a sense of summation and conclusion. The message is not about fixing the past but rather about going into the future. The man has ascended to victory and out of this comes the King, Will—the essence of man.

My future reward is the opportunity to do what I want.

Now that all ten cards are before me, the entire message is revealed.

The reading begins with The Devil card, holding back spiritual/ sexual energy to focus all the soul into action. Dispirited perhaps because the battle of writing this book is over, the soldier must lie down and die.

Three intertwining segments make up the rest of the reading. Knowing and understanding produce the conclusion; whimsical ideas and speculative thoughts allow energies to replenish and forge new directions; victory leads to freedom.

The Two and Three of Swords are of the mind, while the Seven of Cups is of imagination. The three Cup cards represent the lower part of the body and action, as does the Seven of Wands.

The first three cards are about ending. The last seven cards are a unified, integrated message about getting to a place of freedom.

At the end of a reading I ask the subject for questions. Often I am asked, "Will this (the reading) really happen?"

The message of the tarot can be seen as a path that one must walk upon. How long will it take? How fast do you walk? Some people see/hear the message but don't take the advice, never walk upon the path, remain where they are on the earth and never move their soul closer to the light.

Once, many years ago, on a trip to Vienna, my spiritual teacher met Sigmund Freud.

"What is psychology?" my teacher asked the doctor.

"There is a world of the head and a world of the heart," Dr. Freud explained. "Psychology is the science of that schism." Then, looking over his glasses at my teacher, the doctor asked, "And what about you? What is Cabala?"

"There is a world of the head and a world of the heart," agreed my teacher. "Cabala is the bridge."

TABLES OF
CARD ASSOCIATIONS

TABLE OF CARD ASSOCIATIONS FOR MINOR ARCANA

CARD	ATTRIBUTE	ANATOMY	COLOR	PLANET
Ace	Pleasure	Inner Aura	Pure white	Core of Sun
King	Will	Aura	Off-white	Surface of Sun
Queen	Intellect	Head	Silver	Sun
Knight	Emotions	Body	Silver	Sun
Page	Action	Legs	Silver	Sun
Two	Understanding	Left lobe	Gold	Mercury
Three	Knowing	Cerebellum	Brass	Venus
Four	Kindness	Right arm	Blue	Earth
Five	Severity	Left arm	Red	Mars
Six	Beauty/Truth	Torso	Green	Jupiter
Seven	Victory	Right leg	Violet	Saturn
Eight	Splendor	Left leg	Orange	Uranus
Nine	Foundation	Sex	Yellow	Neptune
Ten	Kingship	Mouth	Purple	Pluto

Color and planet associations are inferred from the Zohar.

TABLE OF CARD ASSOCIATIONS FOR MAJOR ARCANA

CARD	ATTRIBUTE	SEFIRA	ANATOMY	KEYWORD
Hanged Man	Pleasure	Keter	Aura	Open-mindedness
Tower	Will	Keter	Aura	Single-mindedness
Emperor	Power of What	Chochma	Right brain	Sight
Empress	Power of What	Chochma	Right brain	Insight
Hermit	Understanding	Binah	Left brain	Hearing
High Priestess	Understanding	Binah	Left brain	Listening
Justice	Knowing	Daat	Cerebellum	Logical knowing
Hierophant	Knowing	Daat	Cerebellum	Intuitive knowing
Sun	Kindness	Chesed	Right arm	Obvious blessing
Star	Kindness	Chesed	Right arm	Subtle blessing
Judgement	Severity	Gevurah	Left arm	Renewal
Death	Severity	Gevurah	Left arm	End of cycle
Magician	Beauty/Truth	Tiferet	Torso	Power of heart wisdom
Fool	Beauty/Truth	Tiferet	Torso	Power of faith
Chariot	Victory	Netzach	Right leg	External strength
Strength	Victory	Netzach	Right leg	Internal strength
Temperance	Splendor	Hod	Left leg	Patience
Moon	Splendor	Hod	Left leg	Letting go
Lovers	Foundation	Yesod	Genitals	Embracing our nature
Devil	Foundation	Yesod	Genitals	Resisting our nature
World	Speech	Malchut	Mouth	Observable "speech" of Creator
Wheel of Fortune	Speech	Malchut	Mouth	Subtle speech of Creator

GLOSSARY

Asiyah (The World of Action). The lowest of the four spiritual worlds; our world is the physical representation of that fourth world.

Atzilut (The World of Emanation). The highest of the four spiritual worlds, corresponding to the soul.

Binah (understanding). The second Sefira, corresponding in the body to the left side of the brain.

Briah (The World of Creation). The second (from the top) of the four worlds, corresponding to thought.

Chaya (gives life). The external manifestation of Will.

Chesed (kindness). The fourth Sefira, corresponding in the body to the lungs. The first of the six emotions.

Chochma (wisdom, or "the power of what"). The first Sefira, corresponding in the body to the right side of the brain.

Daat (knowing). The third Sefira, corresponding in the body to the left side of the brain.

Emet (truth). A statement that does not contradict itself and includes a beginning, middle, and end.

Emunah (faith). Faith expressed through repetitive practice, like that of a craftsman who does not need to think about his actions.

Gemara (learning). A three-hundred-year debate over the *Mishnah* that culminated in the codification of laws dating back 1,800 years.

131

Gevurah (strength). The fifth Sefira, corresponding in the body to the heart.

Hasidim. A branch of orthodox Jews who derive the basis of their practice from the teachings of Baal Shem Tov.

Hod (splendor). The eighth Sefira, corresponding in the body to the left leg.

Keter (crown). Chaos; also describes the two powers essential to life, Pleasure and Will.

Malchut (kingship). The tenth Sefira, representing speech and action.

Midrash (seeking). The middle level of the oral tradition replete with stories and parables.

Mishnah (repetition). The beginning of the oral tradition; short paragraphs, the basis for all Talmudic arguments.

Nefesh (creature). The lowest level of the five parts of the soul, comparable to the feet and legs.

Neshama (Breath of Life). The middle level of the five parts of the soul, conductor of intellect.

Netzach (victory). The seventh Sefira, corresponding in the body to the right leg that strides out.

Ruach (Spirit). The second level of the five parts of the soul, which conducts emotions.

Sefirot (plural—Sefira). One of the ten basic attributes of creation.

Sfat (lookout). Ancient city in northern Israel, known as the home of the cabalists.

Tiferet (beauty). The sixth Sefira, corresponding in the body to the torso. Also known as truth because all limbs of the body connect to the torso.

Torah (teaching). The Five Books of Moses, which relate the history of the earth from the creation of the first two human beings until the death of Moses 2,500 years later. Torah is also used to describe the entirety of Jewish knowledge, both written and oral.

Yachida (Oneness). The highest level of the five parts of the soul, corresponding to pleasure and female.

Yeshiva (house of study). Derived from the the verb meaning "to sit." School for the study of Torah.

Yesod (foundation). The ninth Sefira, corresponding in the body to the genitals; the esoteric as expressed through sexuality and creativity.

Yetzirah (The World of Formation). Third of the four spiritual worlds; spiritual root of all emotions.

YHVH. Highest of the seven names of the Creator whose letters hint at the three states of being—was, is, and will be—a revelation beyond the confines of time.

Yisroel (God wrestlers). The name given to the Jewish people by the Creator; all the Jewish people are known as the children of Yisroel, or Israel.

BOOKS OF RELATED INTEREST

The Kabbalistic Mirror of Genesis
Commentary on the First Three Chapters
by David Chaim Smith

Qabbalistic Magic
Talismans, Psalms, Amulets, and the Practice of High Ritual
by Salomo Baal-Shem
Foreword by Dolores Ashcroft-Nowicki

Kabbalah and the Power of Dreaming
Awakening the Visionary Life
by Catherine Shainberg

The Real Name of God
Embracing the Full Essence of the Divine
by Rabbi Wayne Dosick, Ph.D.

The Secret Doctrine of the Kabbalah
Recovering the Key to Hebraic Sacred Science
by Leonora Leet, Ph.D.

The Kabbalah of the Soul
The Transformative Psychology and Practices of Jewish Mysticism
by Leonora Leet, Ph.D.

The Universal Kabbalah
by Leonora Leet, Ph.D

The Way of Tarot
The Spiritual Teacher in the Cards
by Alejandro Jodorowsky and Marianne Costa

Inner Traditions • Bear & Company
P.O. Box 388
Rochester, VT 05767
1-800-246-8648
www.InnerTraditions.com

Or contact your local bookseller